"This book taught me new ways to pray using the Lord's Prayer as a template for my daily prayer life. I was blessed by the Gospel-centeredness of the book, challenged to pray with more focus and encouraged in my spirit. I have been recommending this book to leaders and pastors in various settings, and I highly recommend this book as an important tool in your prayer arsenal."

Gord Fleming
North American Director
C2C Network

"Most of us refer to this as the Lord's Prayer, which of course it is. Or at a closer look, is it? I believe this is an irresistible prayer that draws the Father ever so close so that He seemingly leans in to hear. Perhaps instead, it should be called the Disciple's Prayer or even better yet, the Model Prayer. Yes, it is this and much more. Ask Sara Maynard of Redleaf Prayer Ministries, she knows. Ask her. Better yet, read about this treasure that she has poured her heart and soul into, read this book and you too will be an answer to the prayers that Jesus prays!"

Dr. James W Goll
God Encounters Ministries
Life Language Trainer, International Speaker and Author, Recording Artist

"This is a book birthed and revealed in prayer. As one saturated by the Kingdom of heaven, Sara's prophetic insights into the Lord's Prayer are like "the owner of a house who brings out of his storeroom new treasures as well as old" (Mt 13:52). Prepare your heart for revival as you rediscover the heart of Jesus in these pages and this prayer. This is not a just a book to read but rather a daily path to walk in the way of Jesus."

Randy Friesen
General Director
MB Mission

"Filled with sound theological insight and practical lessons to live by, 'The Prayer of All Prayers' will draw you deep into a prayer that is much more than something we've learned to memorize. As you read this important book, you will also say that a common prayer—it is not! Sara skillfully awakens us to its relevance and deep meaning that countless souls have discovered over the ages.

Many of us can say that Sara has lived this book over the last few years! She has poured herself, and all her expertise regarding prayer, into these pages to help us re-discover the timelessness of the Lord's Prayer for today."

Rob Parker
Founder and Executive Director
National House of Prayer

"This is a great book! I was so motivated to get back into praying The Lord's Prayer daily as I read it. This is a prayer inspired by God Himself. If we all prayed the whole prayer slowly and deeply every day, I am confident that a great shift would take place—first personally, then in our families, and ultimately in our nations."

Wesley and Stacey Campbell
Authors: *Praying The Bible: The Pathway to Spirituality* &
Praying the Bible: The Book of Prayers

"This book delivers, in a fresh way, the gift that the Lord's Prayer is for us as the church. It is a beautiful extension of Christ's invitation to 'pray like this...' and one that stands to unite the church across traditions and awaken her in profound ways to the power of prayer."

Father Chad Block
Priest, Via Vancouver
Rector, Church of Ascension

"I'll always remember the first time I heard Sara teach on the Lord's Prayer. The revelation she carried changed my whole approach, not only to that prayer, but to prayer. A few years passed, and Sara kept digging, and labouring with it. The thing is, Sara goes for the deep, the real and the practical. She is a no-nonsense prayer practitioner and a passionate lover of truth. So the Lord just keeps opening more of His treasure to her. She writes that the Lord's Prayer is like... "a tall ship, beautiful to look at when sitting at dock, but when the sails are unfurled and the wind begins to blow it's more than an admirable piece of craftsmanship, it becomes a mighty vessel moving with grace, power, and speed. It's a vessel that takes you somewhere!" Well, this book will also take you somewhere, and you'll never regret the journey!"

Alain Caron

Author of *Apostolic Centers - Shifting the Church, Transforming the World*

Leader of the Hodos Network & Le Chemin Apostolic Centre

THE PRAYER OF ALL PRAYERS

FINDING LIFE AND REVIVAL IN THE LORD'S PRAYER

The Prayer of All Prayers

A resource of Cathedral Library

cathedrallibrary.com

Cover design by Melissa D. Baker Nguyen

lostbumblebee.com

Additional copies can be purchased through Redleaf Prayer (redleafprayer.org) or Cathedral Library.

ISBN: 978-1-9994283-0-3

Contents

Foreword

Early in my pastoral ministry I was doing a preaching series entitled 'Spiritual Disciplines from the Gospel of Luke.' When I reached the 11th chapter of that Gospel the words of Jesus challenged me greatly: "Now Jesus was praying in a certain place, and when he finished, one of his disciples said to him, "Lord, teach us to pray, as John taught his disciples." And he said to them, "When you pray, say...."

At that time many young leaders in my congregation were asking me to teach them how to pray. In truth, if there were one thing I would wish to pass onto them it would have been how to have direct contact with God through the discipline of prayer. However, I found their request difficult to answer. I had a desire to teach my congregation to pray but I didn't know how to teach them to pray. Is prayer something so personal that you just have to learn it by yourself? I felt like the pianist who plays only by ear but can't teach others to play.

Luke 11:1ff had a jarring effect on me on three accounts. First, because Jesus was asked the same question – "Lord, teach us to pray" and wasn't lost for an answer. Second, because it seemed clear to the disciples that this was central in the teacher/disciple relationship and not extraneous to it. "Teach us to pray, as John taught his disciples." How little I had done this! And thirdly, because Jesus provided his students with a radically different answer than I had been giving.

To those who were hoping to learn from me the discipline of prayer, never would it have occurred to me to provide them with, what I called, a 'set prayer.' I may have even thought of this as contrary to the very essence of prayer. I could never have even imagined myself saying to my congregation, "When you pray, say..." The two gravest problems were that [1] I had nothing better to offer them, and more serious still [2] why was I against this type of prayer when Christ wasn't? I was so off track.

My response was heartfelt repentance. When people came to me asking, "Teach us to pray" my first instinct, as a minister of Christ, ought to have been to give them Christ's own answer to that question. In the following years I learned that this prayer Jesus provided his disciples, which has become known as 'The Lord's Prayer', played a very important role in the development of the church.

Professor J.I. Packer, in his book "*Growing in Christ*", describes the discipleship process of the early church (called catechesis)[1]. His book outlines the three main tools of early Christian discipleship/catechesis. The Apostles Creed was thought of as the principle expression of orthodox theology. The Ten Commandments was treated as the expression of orthodox morality. And The Lord's Prayer was used as the expression of orthodox spirituality.

Those of us who take our cues from the early centuries of the church love that these three emphases were thought to constitute a thoroughgoing catechesis/discipleship process. This was the case in Holy Scripture. The Epistles of St. Paul cover all three emphases and he moves between them with ease. That is precisely because the Christian revelation has something authoritatively to say about all three areas. Theology, morality, and spirituality are therefore inseparable in the Gospel. There are right things to believe about God, there is a right ethic that is worthy of God, and a right way of relating to God. And the right way of relating to God is revealed to us clearly in The Lord's Prayer.

Because of the Gospel you gain a Father!!! It doesn't get any better

---

1 J. I. Packer, *Growing in Christ* (Wheaton, Ill: Crossway, 1994).

than that. He doesn't have the shortcomings that earthly father's have because he is altogether different from them. He is a Heavenly Father! What kind of Father is he you ask? He is the kind of Father who rules the world! And provides for us! He forgives us when we fail and teaches us to offer the same! He protects us from temptation and keeps us from being ruled by evil!

I am caught up just thinking about it. However, it is not my job to walk you through the many glories of The Lord's Prayer and all of its illustrious Gospel content. That is Sara Maynard's joy.

Sara Maynard is, in my opinion, nothing less than a modern-day Phoebe. In Romans 16:1-2, St. Paul writes, "I commend to you our sister Phoebe, a deaconess of the church at Cenchreae, that you may welcome her in the Lord in a way worthy of the saints." In that same manner, I commend to you Sara Maynard and her book. This dear sister in Christ leads a life devoted to prayer like few I know. In this book she is doing so much more than inspiring us to pray, calling us to prayer, or underscoring for us the importance of prayer. Sara is going to show us HOW to pray. And she is going to do that using the very same way that Jesus taught the original disciples to pray. The word 'orthodox' means 'true to the original.' This then is an orthodox approach to prayer because it takes us back to the original, time tested way that prayer was taught from the very origin and by the very Originator of our Faith.

I expect that this book will find an appeal with two different audiences. There will be those who have grown up in the liturgical church, prayed The Lord's Prayer weekly if not daily, and yet hadn't realized the enormity of the gift they had been given. The second group will be those who come from non-liturgical churches. Perhaps you have been hesitant to pray any prayer you didn't spontaneously create. But the Holy Spirit has been at work intimating to you that there may be more treasure in other parts of the Body of Christ than you have appreciated, and that it is now time for you to lay hold of that treasure.

It seems to me that praying The Lord's Prayer holds potential beyond what we can see. By this I refer to the potential of making one again a church that is fragmented. The liturgical church praying with the non-liturgical church. The contemporary church praying, as it were, with the ancient church. Nations of Christians praying with other nations of Christians. If we were left to our own devices we would find it a difficult exercise to settle upon prayers that every branch of the Church could agree upon. However, praying through a prayer that our common Lord himself gave us, and praying it in common – together – is something we most certainly can do. May God work through this book to further the high calling of prayer, to further orthodox, gospel-centered praying, and to further the unity that comes by praying together.

+Todd Atkinson Eastertide 2018

Bishop of Via Apostolica

www.viaapostolica.ca

Our Father in heaven, hallowed be your name.

Your kingdom come, your will be done,

on earth as it is in heaven.

Give us this day our daily bread.

And forgive us our trespasses

as we forgive those who have
trespassed against us.

And lead us not into temptation,
but deliver us from evil.

For yours is the kingdom and
the power and the glory,

for ever and ever.

Amen.

Introduction

Picture this setting with me…

Dark, lush woods, dense with hemlock, pine and cedar trees, creating an intricate texture of emerald greens and browns. These, like giants on guard, stand gripping the rocky crags with their gnarled roots as if the granite was a miser's treasure. A little further over, the scene opens to reveal jagged, mossy rock and then suddenly your eye drops, taking in the drama and power of the ravine and its thundering river below.

Across this chasm is strung a seemingly frail foot bridge, being tossed about in the updraft of the spray.

There is often a marked difference between what we declare we believe and what we truly entrust the weight of our life to. Yet authentic faith looks like crossing a wild ravine: faith has no safety net nor a "Plan B". We can look at a foot bridge over a chasm, research its strength, hear others proclaim that it is easily able to sustain our weight, and become intellectually convinced. But the truth of our belief is tested when we face the choice to cross the bridge ourselves. Do we believe in the integrity of the bridge to the point of complete trust—which looks like great risk—or do we discreetly look for another route across the ravine?

This gap between what we think we believe, and what we *actually* believe in our hearts is a reality for all of us. Thankfully, Jesus is well aware of our need to grow in our authentic faith and trust in him. He doesn't shame us for having this inconsistency between what we mentally believe is true, he understands that we are in process, that we are "but dust"[2] and so he works gently but unrelentingly, calling us to believe in him, in his character, and in his word.

This dichotomy of belief is the situation most of us find ourselves in when we think about the Lord's Prayer. If asked what is the most important prayer, the prayer of all prayers, many, if not most Christians would quickly and correctly answer the Lord's Prayer. If asked whether Jesus knew what he was doing when he gave it to us and instructed us to pray it, there would be an enthusiastic chorus of, "Yes! Of course He did!" We all get this answer right on the exam. Gold stars all around!

However, if this same group of Christians was asked how many of them pray it daily, pray it deeply, and keep praying it even through the moments when it seems dry, my guess is that the room would grow awkwardly silent. There would be a few exceptions, but I suspect the majority would confess that even though they believe it is a vital prayer, it's not been something that has brought *them* life. Perhaps they tried it for a season but abandoned the discipline as it felt religious, empty, and not nearly as satisfying as spontaneous, conversational prayer that flowed from their hearts.

Others might say that they also tried this prayer, but quickly came to the conclusion that Jesus never *really* intended us to pray it daily, but rather intended it to be a general catalog of the scope of topics for prayer. His intention was, once we got these under our belt and understood that these were good directions to pray, we could move on to more sophisticated and interesting prayer.

It's possible that there could be a third group that faithfully recites the Lord's Prayer daily as a devout habit. However, if asked, they might not be able to explain what they are actually requesting when they pray it, nor could they authentically confirm that they had faith-filled

---

2 Ps 103:14

expectations that their prayers were being answered. In fact, they might admit that they prayed it as a bit of a carry-over from how they'd been trained or raised, just in case what they were taught was true and this was a way get God's blessing.

But what is missing in all of these scenarios is a confident belief that this is the prayer that Jesus gave us to pray—and that it works. A confident belief that we can put the full weight of our prayer life upon it, and that it can become the cornerstone that teaches us to pray, awakens us in prayer, draws us closer to God in intimacy and discipleship, and guides us into the most outstanding answers to prayer we could conceive. It's like we are all vocal advocates of the strength of the foot bridge, while still standing on the bank, lacking the confidence to route our daily commute across it.

In spite of all of this, there remains a small and growing number that have chosen to walk faithfully in the power and revelation of praying the Lord's Prayer. This book is not revealing anything new, but rather advocating for this ancient revelation—that the Lord's Prayer works—in the hope that with it being rediscovered many more will join this movement.

As a leader of prayer at a national level in Canada for over seventeen years, I have followed the trends and teachings on prayer in pursuit of more and more effective intercession. The teaching on conversational prayer, prophetic prayer, spiritual warfare, spiritual mapping, harp and bowl style worship and prayer, praying apostolic prayers, fasting, travailing, blessing Israel and even praying the prayer of Jabez are all teachings that I have sat under, and many of them I have taught myself. In all of this, I and the others who have walked a similar journey have looked for two crucial things in prayer:

First—an authentic connection with God: the spiritual encounter of God's presence; life-giving communion with him.

Second - answers: the change he brings as he intervenes in our lives, our communities, our families, and our nations; the evidence of the hand of God moving and working in us, through us, and all around us.

While both of these desires have been met in measure, there has always been a sense that there was still more we hadn't tapped into, and that prayer was meant to be richer. Perhaps you can relate to this longing for more. Certainly, as I have travelled and connected with the Canadian prayer movement and walked with leaders from other nations, I've seen everywhere, an expressed desire for prayer to have greater impact.

This desire for more impact has fostered, over the years, much teaching of new revelation with "keys" for effective prayer, yet most have not been based on the Lord's Prayer. While Jesus has certainly used these teachings and the practices that they have fostered, this longing for prayer to impact us, and impact the world around us remains. It's a longing that invites us to look deeper, to draw closer and to consider more carefully how Jesus himself taught us to pray.

MY STORY

It was the summer of 2012 when the Lord launched our house of prayer into an intense, intercessory focus on revival. We met for prayer many times a day, contending for a revival that would renew the Church and sweep millions into the kingdom. We fasted, we prophesied, we gathered others with the same fire in their bones and fervently prayed together. During this time the Lord gave us a mandate to research and write about the historical revivals in the Canadian Church, considering common factors and identifying what we could learn from these, our forefathers, who saw such extraordinary moves of God sweep across our land in previous generations.

The stories of these Canadian revivals were compelling and the Lord led me to assemble them in a book, "Canadian Mantles of Revival," which was published in January 2014. It fueled our hunger for revival and our commitment to pray for it. Later, when the Lord spoke to me and called me to pray the Lord's Prayer deeply and daily (although I didn't realize it until much later) it was actually an answer, in part, to these years of intercession.

He was responding to our cry for revival, by giving us the Lord's Prayer.

I have to confess that even though I responded in obedience to this assignment, I initially had no expectation of the life and revival praying the Lord's Prayer would bring to me. I anticipated it would be an additional, daily "to do", simply because the Father said so, perhaps to build character. So, when the prayer opened up extravagant, presence-filled rivers of life, I was totally stunned. What had been disregarded as either dusty, religious liturgy, or the "beginner's prayer", was in fact the greatest wellspring of communion, intercession, and revival I'd ever encountered. My prayer life, once full of contending for revival, now included humble repentance for not giving the Lord's Prayer its rightful place for so long.

It became apparent that I was not alone. Many others have skimmed over the Lord's Prayer, minimizing its rightful place and honour. In fact, this perspective is rampant. This strange reality should make us wonder if there is a demonic strategy involved in keeping the Church from this powerhouse prayer. If so, it would be highly strategic because of how the Lord's Prayer could radically change us, unite us, and launch us into the most glorious revival we've seen.

The enemy's lies and accusations have been subtly but maliciously slandering the Lord's Prayer, convincing us that praying it would be fruitless, boring, and dry, filling us with dead religion. These demonic impressions have coloured our emotional response to the Lord's Prayer, to the point that many believers (of course, not all) particularly in the Charismatic and Pentecostal streams, avoid it altogether, like that foot bridge across the chasm. We've had no confidence that this prayer would be life-giving.

Some have zeroed in on the phrase, "Let your kingdom come and your will be done on earth as it is in heaven," and have used this fragment as a substitute for the whole. There is nothing at all wrong with praying this one segment—it's full of truth and life and the will of God! However, when removed from the context of the whole prayer it can be easily distorted. If we only pray the sections of this prayer that we most naturally respond to, we are not allowing it to disciple us. Rather, we are actually avoiding God's will and asserting our own.

As I began to pray the Lord's Prayer daily the encounters it opened up with the Lord overwhelmed me. After several months I began to encourage my friends and fellow ministers into this practice, with a mixed response. Some were one hundred percent on the same page: they jumped in and have stayed engaged with the Lord's Prayer, finding it has opened up glorious new levels of communion, and rapid answers to their prayers. Others were slightly wary, concerned that I was perhaps being influenced by a religious spirit. Still others said, "Well, I tried that. I used to pray the Lord's Prayer when Larry Lea's teaching[3] came out in the '80s, but it became too much work." Perhaps you too are skeptical. Could I encourage you to at least journey through this book, take a new look at the power of this prayer before dismissing the practice of praying it daily. I think you will be surprised.

THE SPIRIT'S ENDORSEMENT

After praying the Lord's Prayer deeply, daily, for about four months, something strange began to occur. I would often walk as I prayed and on these prayer walks I started seeing doves. Now, I live on the west coast of Canada, in a region where we commonly see spectacular eagles circling overhead or perched on trees. We also have seagulls, crows, robins, and sparrows in abundance. But in this region, before this time, I can't remember *ever* seeing a dove. And it wasn't just once, or twice, but a regular occurrence that as I walked and prayed, I would look up and see a dove perched in the tree or power line above me. They would appear alone or at times in a pair, often cooing, and even following me as I walked.

Not wanting to be super-spiritual, I rejoiced in this, but also wondered if the explanation was simply that the route I frequently walked

3 Larry Lea, *Could You Not Tarry One Hour? Learning the Joy of Prayer* (Altamonte Springs, FL:Creation House,1987).

had become the territory of this pair of doves. Did their appearance really have something to do with the Lord's Prayer? Still I kept seeing them, and later that year, while on a trip to Wales seeking the Lord for revival, I was again walking and praying the Lord's Prayer when a familiar cooing sound caught my attention. I turned to see a beautiful dove perched on a little cottage not more than ten feet away from me. The name on the cottage was Bethel (meaning House of God). Clearly God was speaking.

A few weeks later I was visiting my Bishop, his family, and church in Lethbridge, Alberta. I continued my daily practice of walking and praying and there too, a dove appeared! These softly cooing birds suddenly seemed to be everywhere! By this time, I was completely convinced that God was speaking, but what was he saying?

There are two major passages of scripture where doves are featured. In the Old Testament, Noah sent out a dove to see if there was a resting place to be found after the flood.[4] The second important occurrence is found in the New Testament, when the Holy Spirit descended in the form of a dove as a visible endorsement of Jesus at his baptism. The Holy Spirit resting upon Jesus affirmed what the Father was declaring: *"This is my Beloved Son, with whom I am well pleased"*[5]. With these passages in mind, I believe the Lord is revealing two things. First, that the Holy Spirit is resting with new emphasis on the Lord's Prayer, and second, that there is a "Well pleased!" heavenly endorsement of the Church freshly embracing it.

It became apparent that this sign was not only about my personal journey in the Lord's Prayer. As I eventually shared some of the dove stories, I discovered many people had experienced exactly the same thing. After they had begun praying the Lord's Prayer in a more intentional way, doves appeared consistently, sometimes even nesting in their yards.

The other remarkable thing that began to happen was the stunning increase in answers to prayer, to the point that my life and ministry

4 Gen 8:8
5 Mt 3:16

have completely changed. I'm not suggesting that the Lord's Prayer is a magic formula to get spiritual power. It is, however, a way to draw into greater union with and surrender to Jesus, so that we are abiding in him, and his words are abiding in us. From this place of union, as Jesus teaches us, we can ask for whatever we wish and it will be done for us.[6]

What I am *not* saying, and earnestly hope you do not hear in the tone of this book, is that praying the Lord's Prayer is the only acceptable way to pray. Certainly this is not true, nor is it what scripture teaches us. The New Testament records numerous prayers of the Apostles and while they prayed the Lord's Prayer (and it is resounding through their written prayers), they go beyond its words. Prayer, led by the Spirit, spontaneously, passionately, flows from their hearts. The Psalms also contain powerful prayers that Jesus himself prayed. Praying the Lord's Prayer is not meant to be a restriction, but rather a way for us to be grounded into the root of prayer. What I *am* saying, is that for all of us, this prayer of all prayers should be the cornerstone, even the centrepiece, of our prayer life.

Hundreds of books, essays, and commentaries have been written on the Lord's Prayer. Since the time of Christ, theologians and preachers have dug deep into the rich layers of meaning in this prayer, expounding beautiful revelation. This book has no ambition to stand alongside these classics. It is not my goal to add to the corporate honouring of the theology of the prayer. This will always be a worthy endeavour, as it teaches us the heart of the gospel as well as the nature of God. But others have done that well. Instead, the goal of this book is to testify, and to activate many (perhaps you) in applying themselves to the wonderful, transformative practice of daily praying the Lord's Prayer.

This book then, is a testimony that praying the prayer Jesus gave us to pray and instructed us to pray, is good. Actually, it's far beyond good, it's amazing. This book is a testimony to the way this prayer will change our lives if we will apply ourselves to it. It's also, I hope, a practical

6 Jn 15:7

on-ramp for those who desire to step further into it and find the glory and the blessing that it was meant to give us.

As well as testifying, this book is written as a resource. Each phrase of the Lord's Prayer is explored, along with many applications as to how prayer can flow from that one phrase. I've also provided a list of scriptures at the end of each chapter which relate to these phrases, to add depth and understanding. When meditated on in conjunction with the Lord's Prayer, these scriptures are a goldmine, and will add tremendously to the faith and authority you move in as you pray this prayer. As this is ultimately a corporate prayer, you might want to read this book with others in a small group and grow in it together. To assist with this, I've included group discussion questions at the end of each chapter, hopefully pointing you towards some of the key thoughts of each chapter.

How we value this prayer, and the conviction we bring to praying it, will greatly influence how much we gain from it. If we consider the Lord's Prayer to be just one of many equal options on the smorgasbord table of prayer—a beautiful dish, yet with all the other dishes vying for the attention of our taste buds—we're tempted to just take a nibble and move on. With this perspective, we won't gain its full benefits. Without truly valuing and engaging in this prayer, it will remain for us a hidden treasure buried in a field.[7] In addition, if we hold all the variety of prayer styles and focuses being promoted today as equal to the instruction in prayer that Jesus himself gave us we are not allowing him to disciple us; we are in charge, doing what is right in our own eyes.

Think for a moment of a recreational runner being coached to be a top notch athlete. He doesn't know how to get to this level on his own, so he submits to his coach. Even if he doesn't understand the necessity of the drills and exercises the coach gives him to do, he still trusts and follows the regimen. He is a disciple. Over time, the wisdom of the coach becomes evident as the runner emerges with strength, endurance and skill far beyond what he could have achieved independently. If he

---

7 Mt 13:44

had set up his own training regimen, he certainly would have fallen short of what the coach could have helped him achieve. In the same way, we are going to the expert—the Son of God—who created us and created prayer. The Lord's Prayer is not an optional approach that works for some—it is how Jesus taught us all to pray.

We need to approach the Lord's Prayer with wholehearted faith that it will be good, that it will be fruitful and that it will remain a glorious blessing, leading us into the fullness of what God has for us in prayer. As in the picture of the foot bridge, we have to be willing to trust that the Lord's Prayer is the prayer vehicle that is great enough to carry the primary weight of our lives, needs and longings to the Father. By trusting it, we are trusting Jesus, as the one who knows better than we how to pray.

Chapter One

THE DISCIPLES' PRAYER

Sometimes when we read the New Testament, we forget that it's not just God speaking directly to us, but that he is speaking through the voice of the Apostles and those whom the Apostles discipled. We forget that these writings were in part a response to the Great Commission[8] (the call to not just make converts, but disciples), which Jesus first gave to his followers.

The disciples, and more particularly, the Apostles who led them, were all Jesus left behind. He left no writings or manuals or organizations; he left a few hundred followers and eleven leaders whom he had personally chosen and mentored. To these ones, Jesus entrusted the role of laying the foundation of the Church and passing on his message (the Good News), in all its fullness, redemption and power. It's easy for us to forget the reality that all that Jesus set in motion was faithfully stewarded and passed along through the Apostles, and we are being discipled into this through the scriptures. We live in a video generation where life is documented by cameras everywhere and uploaded for universal access, so it's easy to think of the record of scripture (especially the gospels) as a neutral, video documentary. But this is not the case. Every

---

8 Mt 28:19

word has been inspired by the Holy Spirit, but the writers, especially of the gospels, had purpose in including specific stories and teachings, and their purpose was to disciple us.

With that in mind, when we examine Luke 11 (a primary passage where the Lord's Prayer is taught), we are indeed being discipled by Jesus, but through Luke, a disciple of Paul. Why does this matter? It's because every detail he writes is purposeful; what's included, what's repeated, what's highlighted. All of this leads to a greater revelation of Jesus if we will have ears to hear and posture ourselves as disciples (learners).

Luke introduces Jesus' teaching on prayer like this:

> *"Now Jesus was praying in a certain place, and when he finished, one of his disciples said to him, 'Lord, teach us to pray…'" Lk 11:1a*

This is not a random or casual request for prayer instruction. Luke wants us to grasp the impact Jesus' prayer life had upon his disciples. There had never been anyone who prayed like Jesus, with this singular level of anointing, intimacy, authority and presence of God resting on his prayer. If you or I had been there, we too would have voiced our longing to be taught to pray like this. Jesus was the first man since Adam who was praying with a pure, unhindered, unobstructed vision of the Father; with pure faith and pure motives. We can only imagine the level of the presence of God that rested on him as he prayed. The disciples were witnessing the Gate of Heaven.[9]

He responds to their request to be mentored in his kind of prayer by giving them a simple instruction, "When you pray, say… " [10] (or as Matthew records: "Pray then like this…"[11]). What Jesus knew and what the gospel writers are passing along to us, is that even though his response was simple, it was complete. The Disciples' Prayer is not a beginner's prayer that we will eventually outgrow; these simple petitions

---

9 Gen 28:17, Jn 1:51

10 Lk 11:2

11 Mt 6:9

are the path that leads to the same quality of prayer life that Jesus enjoyed with the Father.

If we are Jesus' disciples we will follow his instructions even if they don't seem to make sense to us, even if they're not the way we would choose. This is the reason we ask to be taught anything; because we don't know how to do it as well as someone else. In John's gospel, Jesus explained that not only would following his teaching (which includes of course, his teaching on prayer) *prove* that we were his disciples, but it would lead us into extraordinary blessing. He taught us that if we clung to his teaching, dwelt in his teaching, that this teaching would change us. It would fill us with truth in a way that brings us into beautiful, expansive, freedom.[12]

In this sense, praying the Lord's Prayer becomes a way to affirm our discipleship, and to taste, in a small but growing way, the rich communion of prayer that Jesus has with the Father.

This invitation to discipleship and communion is being freshly extended today and every day. If we haven't responded to it before, or feel that we've responded without understanding, intentionality or faith, the invitation to step in deeper and embrace this prayer is still wide open to us. It's never too late, and for any who come to Jesus to be discipled, there is no reproach.

THE EARLY CHURCH

The first disciples and Apostles took the words of Jesus to heart and earnestly embraced the Lord's Prayer as their own. They simply believed that the Lord had commanded them to pray this prayer every day, and so it was their practice to do so, using it as the core element of their three daily times of prayer. It was the heartbeat of their prayer life, as they flowed in communion and intercession.

They considered it a foundational part of their personal devotional life, but also considered it "the Prayer of the Church". It was always

---

12 Jn 8:32

prayed corporately when they gathered on Sundays. The revelation that they were praying to their Father, their dear Abba, as children, and as siblings overwhelmed them. This was the Family's Prayer.

We might look at this lifestyle of prayer and judge it to be legalistic, but for the early Church it was life. They held the Lord's Prayer in highest reverence, even awe. They considered it to be the perfect prayer, the prayer of God, to God. When the early Church Fathers wrote about the Lord's Prayer, in their commentaries and sermons, they spoke of how people trembled as they prayed it; a stark contrast to how casually the Lord's Prayer is prayed today.

In its first centuries in particular, the Church continually referred to the Lord's Prayer as being full of mystery and power. In his exhaustive study on the use of the Lord's Prayer in the early Church, Dr. Roy Hammerling reflects, "The amount of praise that the early Christian authors showered upon the mystery and power of the Lord's Prayer is indeed at times something that strikes the modern reader as unexpected."[13]

Hammerling goes on to explain how all the prominent Church Fathers considered the Lord's Prayer as central in their lives and exceedingly precious. He writes:

> "Ambrose, the renowned fourth-century bishop of Milan, passionately loved the church and what he considered to be its immeasurable treasures. The great wealth of the church for Ambrose, of course, did not reside in the tangible possession of magnificent buildings, gold-plated crosses, and other ornaments of the worship space, but in Jesus and his priceless words.
>
> The heart of Jesus' teaching, for Ambrose, as it was for many early authors, was the Lord's Prayer. Ambrose even likened the Lord's Prayer to a 'pearl' of great value."[14]

The early believers intimately encountered Christ as they prayed

13 Roy Hammerling, *The Lord's Prayer in the Early Church, The Pearl of Great Price (*New York: Palgrave Macmillan, 2010), 4.

14 Hammerling, *The Lord's Prayer in the Early Church*, 3.

his words. They saw their prayers wondrously answered as the gospel advanced against all odds to become the leading faith of the entire Roman empire, breaking in everywhere. It was an unstoppable advance, moving in power to transform lives, accompanied by marvellous signs and wonders.

Because the whole Church prayed the same prayer every day, regardless of where they were or their personal situations, this prayer, (along with the weekly celebration of the Lord's Table) became the heart of their expression of unity. United intercession kept their hearts knit together as they pulled for the advance of the gospel wherever they found themselves.

THE WHOLE CHURCH

As we embark on a renewed emphasis on the Lord's Prayer, we are joining in unity with the historic Church. Our intercession through the Lord's Prayer is agreeing with theirs, adding to the powerful, unstoppable, torrent of contending for God's will for individuals, the Church and the nations. It's as if praying this prayer gathers us into an Upper Room-type experience, transcending time and distance, fully united and praying with the Church in one accord. It's not just the early Church with their radical disciples and martyrs that we are agreeing with, it's the desert fathers, the monks and mystics, the reformers and revivalists, the church planters, intercessors and heroic missionaries throughout the centuries. Our prayers add an "Amen!" to theirs.

Those that have died in Christ are not dead, but remain with him in heaven, waiting for the final resurrection. These are the great cloud of witnesses, who cheer us on.[15] They are a part of our spiritual family, and we are, in part, the result of their prayers. How wonderful to unite with what they gave themselves to in intercession and carry on the cry for the kingdom of God to come in fullness.

But it is not just the historic Church that we unite with, and we

---

15 Heb 12:1

don't pray the Lord's Prayer out of a sentimental duty. In this hour of Church history, while there are countless denominations in the body of Christ (countless, because new ones are springing up all the time), this remains a prayer that unites us all. The Lord's Prayer is the one prayer that every denomination is wholeheartedly committed to pray; it is the one prayer that we can all completely, unreservedly agree with. As Jesus builds the Church into perfect unity, the Lord's Prayer will provide a way for those that have been estranged and suspicious of one another to open their hearts, the first step of relationship.

We may still stand opposed and wrestling through theological issues, but when we open our hearts in prayer to address our dear Abba, we hear the common longings and love expressed across this diverse and fractured family. As we listen to each other pray, by the power of the Spirit the reality that we are family hits home. When hearts connect, it creates an even greater urgency to resolve needless divisions. There is no other prayer that we can all earnestly and wholeheartedly engage with; no other prayer we all call our own. Cyprian, the third century Bishop of Carthage, taught that, "The central function of the Lord's Prayer was to bind the Church together in unity".[16] How wonderful that Jesus continues to use the prayer he gave us as a tool to call us back together and so fulfill his prayer of John 17, that we would be one.

It is not just across the denominations that the Lord's Prayer unifies, it is across all the nations, people groups and languages. From the entire body of Christ around the globe, this prayer is prayed every day, every hour of the day. This creates an unceasing offering of incense, in the form of the Lord's Prayer rising from the nations of the earth. How glorious to be a part of this and join with its powerful impact on the earth!

We pray the Lord's Prayer because it's the prayer he gave us to pray and we are his disciples. We also pray it because it's the prayer of unity with the global and historic Church, but there are still more reasons.

A SPIRITUAL PLUMBLINE

---

16 Hammerling, *The Lord's Prayer in the Early Church*, 2010.

The Lord's Prayer is unique in its ability to connect us with the Father, aligning us with his will in times of confusion, chaos, suffering and spiritual warfare, or when the flood of darkness obscures our spiritual bearings. But equally, in times of abundance, blessing and celebration, it holds us in the holy posture of surrender and dependence. It steadies our focus on the eternal things when temporal joys tempt us to shift our gaze. It both holds us unwavering in the storm and keeps us from pride and independence in the days abounding with blessings.

The Lord's Prayer is a path to daily, sustainable, personal revival, if we will take it. This path leads us through renewed surrender, intimate dependence, crying out for his Spirit to fill us, repenting of all known sin, releasing forgiveness and declaring his victory. This journey touches all the major issues essential to maintaining a vibrant and revived communion with the Father.

Anyone can wander from the place of first love and become cold, distant, self-absorbed, fearful, anxious, discouraged or unbelieving. Praying the Lord's Prayer daily nips these and other wandering tendencies in the bud before they lead us into deeper places of darkness, becoming serious issues for us to overcome.

We also find a clear-eyed sense of perspective and proportion as we consistently pray this prayer. The greatness of God overshadows our problems and struggles, putting them in their place. His love, tenderness and affirmation of us as his beloved children keeps us in confidence and faith. The segment of the Prayer that bring us to repentance for sin, and the "Lead me not into temptation" petition, work together to give us a biblical perspective on our weakness, reminding us to stay sensitive to the conviction of the Spirit. The Lord's Prayer reminds us that the Father expects frequent repentance will be needed in any Christian's lifestyle.

These are just a few examples of how the Lord's Prayer secures us in a biblical posture, poised for communion, fruitfulness, and joy. We'll explore these and other examples more deeply as we delve into the prayer phrase by phrase in the coming chapters.

A PRAYER THAT MATURES

The Lord's Prayer is a continual plumbline for our lives in Christ, but it is also an extremely effective discipleship tool. It moves us into a healthy, biblical, perspective, but then as we pray it through, the Holy Spirit has time and access to our hearts allowing him to minister to whatever area of our life is in need of strengthening, encouragement or correction.

In these days discipleship is a tremendous challenge for the Western Church. We may not find it so hard to create an energetic Sunday church experience and attract a crowd, especially if it requires no more from the people than showing up, primarily as consumers, for sixty to ninety minutes. The struggle begins when a church asks for more, such as volunteering or joining a small group. These steps toward being more engaged require increased commitment and here the crowd thins. But the further step into authentic discipleship where our lives are called to imitate Jesus is even less popular. We are a highly independent people and tend to back away or become defensive as soon as areas of our lives are addressed in a manner that creates discomfort or requires change. Of course, there will always be many earnest Christians who are wholehearted and zealous to become more like Jesus, but many more church-goers just want to walk with Jesus as a friend, rather than serve him as their Lord.

The early Church also had challenges with discipleship. They were expanding into new ground with a kingdom world-view, so radically different on every level, from the paganism the Gentile nations were steeped in. The Lord's Prayer became one of the primary discipleship tools for the nascent Church.

It not only revived the hearts of new converts, it was used by God to renew their minds. The Lord's Prayer became a theological anchor against the continual flood of false teaching and paganism. It was taught universally in their catechism, their preparation for baptism. In 390 AD, the Apostles Creed was crafted and stood beside the Lord's Prayer as the two foundational theological statements of the Church.

Today we live in a post-Christian culture where the dominant worldview is secular liberalism, New Age spirituality is everywhere and Eastern thought has quietly entered the mainstream. Much like our early Church brothers and sisters, we can't assume that new believers who come to faith, do so with an essentially Christian worldview. No, there is much more that is needed in this hour. It is imperative that the Lord's Prayer be returned to the central role it held in the early Church's discipleship so that we can once again walk in the power and mystery it brings, but also so our lives will be firmly anchored in the gospel, as secular ideologies and waves of deception again crash upon the Church.

Building a gospel-centred, biblical world-view is an important part of discipleship, but all true transformation begins in the heart. The issues of life flow from the heart, not the head. Knowing what is right, without our hearts being discipled, won't automatically lead to living rightly and has the propensity to lead to shame and hopelessness.

In contrast, praying the Lord's Prayer deeply and daily creates a discipled heart. This is a heart that knows intimately the path of delighting in God as Father, yielding to him, putting his kingdom first, forgiving, trusting, and receiving his presence. By agreeing with the words of his prayer daily, our hearts begin to come alive under them and they become more and more our heartbeat, our theme song. We own them, they become in a greater measure, our earnest desire. Every day as we pray, sometimes with exuberance and fiery faith, other times with emptiness and weakness, we are lining up our lives and striking the ground again and again for Jesus and his kingdom, in us and through us.

How much more easily discipleship and maturity in Christ flow when our lifestyle includes praying the Lord's Prayer daily. Upon this prepared and fertilized ground, the seeds of biblical teaching immediately spring up and bear much fruit. With the Lord's Prayer creating a place for the Lord to daily minister to us, speak to us, strengthen us, cleanse and correct us, we have a path of discipleship that is not only accelerated, but which addresses the hidden issues that only the Father can know.

A PRAYER THAT IS ANSWERED

Lastly the prayer is crucial to pray because it will be answered.

We are called to be a people of prayer. Jesus declared that his house would be known as a house of prayer, where all nations could be welcomed into his presence and commune with him. His house would be where all nations would pray.[17] However, in the Western Church, there is rampant prayerlessness. In broad strokes, prayer is what we do as a last resort, and even then we don't do it very well! There are exceptions to this, pockets of wonderfully prayerful communities, along with many individuals who have deep and rich prayer lives. Yet still, prayerlessness is much more the norm and with it comes a sense of inadequacy and shame over our lack.

Why don't we pray?

In the last seventeen years of teaching on prayer, I have found the most common reason that people don't make time for prayer or build it into their lives, is that at their deepest place of belief, they don't actually expect God to respond. They have experienced more unanswered prayer than answered and the path to changing that reality seems a complete mystery. If you asked if the Father answers prayer, they would say "Yes", eagerly offering supporting scriptures and testimonies. But when pressed with further inquiry, they would gradually admit that prayer isn't what marks their lives, because they rarely see answers.

When we pray the Lord's Prayer, with the leading and empowering of the Spirit, we begin to live in the realm of answered prayer. This quickly becomes a place that we never want to leave, as prayer becomes an authentic connection to heaven's wisdom, resources, life, and power that changes our reality.

There are three main features of prayers that are answered. They are simply:

---

17 Isa 56:7

A. Faith is involved
B. The request is aligned with God's will
C. The prayer perseveres until fulfillment

Praying the Lord's Prayer daily is the easiest way for these features to abound in our prayer lives.

Prayer of Faith

All that we receive from God we receive by grace, though faith.[18] This includes salvation and all that pertains to the kingdom. Faith is essential. Faith is built upon the revelation of who God is, his character, nature, attributes. As we see more clearly who he is, his word becomes authoritative in our hearts and we trust what he says.

Praying through the Lord's Prayer begins with the reminder that God is our Father, so this should resolve any niggling doubts about his heart toward us. He is the perfect, good and kind Father, who cares for every need with tenderness and mercy. As we pray, we are reminded that we are praying the very words Jesus gave us to pray, so our confidence for bold asking soars. Finally, because we are praying in such an absolutely biblical way, the Holy Spirit will often quicken many other scriptures that line up with the prayer, strengthening our faith even more.

God's Will

In order for a prayer to be answered, it must also be in line God's will. The outline of the Prayer continually presents us with the heart of his will, and even though our desires, hopes, and will are fully expressed, they become shaped by his. If we allow this discipling of our desires, we will find that our prayers become more and more like his. Praying like this will bring a resonance from the Holy Spirit, a sense of heaven's endorsement on what we have asked for, fortifying our faith even more.

18 Eph 2:8

Additionally, the Holy Spirit will often reveal a specific application of God's will as we pray. In this way, our discernment and revelation will grow, enabling us to pray very effectively.

Perseverance

The key to perseverance is not grit and stubborn will but love for God. We pray to commune with him and we pray because we are passionate about what matters most to him. We won't let go of either of these—ever. The Lord's Prayer feeds and affirms this perseverance because he endorses so strongly the practice of praying this prayer with his presence and his word. When we keep encountering the Father in prayer, it's not difficult to return to pray again the next day, and the day after that!

Staying in alignment with God's will, full of robust faith and persevering in prayer through times of glory and times of struggle is so much easier when using the Lord's Prayer as a format and guide. Without it, while we desire the leading of the Spirit, we struggle with merely following the stream of emotion at the surface of our hearts, or the drift of our distracted thoughts.

This Disciples' Prayer is indeed a pearl of great price. It's worthy of our trust and our committed obedience. It's worthy to the degree that we would set aside other forms and practices of prayer (perhaps for a time) in order to establish this Prayer of All Prayers as the centrepiece of our prayer lives.

GROUP DISCUSSION QUESTIONS:

1. In what ways has your upbringing or church experience impacted how you've valued the Lord's Prayer?
2. Jesus has given us the Lord's Prayer, to be prayed regularly by all Christians—how does this make you feel?
3. Could you suggest some ways that you feel regularly praying the Lord's Prayer would build up your personal prayer life? What could this look like if applied to your church's corporate prayer times?

Chapter Two

HOW TO PRAY THE LORD'S PRAYER

We've discussed how building our prayer lives around the Lord's Prayer has so many benefits and is truly the mark of one who is being discipled by Jesus in prayer.

But praying the Lord's Prayer involves much more than praying the fifty-seven words that he gave us. It's also taking into consideration the manner in which we are to pray them. Praying has never been just saying the right things. The Lord has never been interested in simple lip-service. He has always intended prayer to be a primary place where our heart would connect with his.

We know this because of the context in which Jesus teaches the Lord's Prayer. In both Matthew and Luke's gospels, it is surrounded by Jesus' teaching on how to pray. He teaches about faith, humility, persistence, how to address God, and more. Then in the Lord's Prayer, he outlines both the flow of prayer and the topics, as a structure that can be used in any setting and in any age. But both the how to pray (found in the context) and the what to pray (the Lord's Prayer) are part of the same teaching, and need to be understood together. With this in mind, this chapter will focus on the tremendous importance of the surrounding verses, and all they teach us about ensuring we don't end up praying empty words in a religious ritual. Finally, we will look at the intention for this prayer to be used as a framework that the Holy Spirit leads us through, inspiring us and directing us to pray in accordance with his will.

IN CONTEXT

We'll begin with the context of the Lord's Prayer in Matthew's gospel[19] where Jesus, in the verses immediately before and after the Lord's Prayer, gives us some critically important instructions. I'll highlight five of these.

A. NOT FOR SHOW Mt 6:5,6

> *"And when you pray, you must not be like the hypocrites. For they love to stand and pray in the synagogues and at the street corners, that they may be seen by others. Truly, I say to you, they have received their reward. But when you pray, go into your room and shut the door and pray to your Father who is in secret. And your Father who sees in secret will reward you."*

Jesus taught a lifestyle of prayer that is primarily a personal, private activity, flowing naturally out of our union and love for God. It's a place of communion, fellowship and daily abiding. It's this activity, more than any other, that illustrates our belief that without him, we can do nothing.[20]

As he taught this radical, relational style of prayer, Jesus was correcting the prevailing practice among the Pharisees, for whom prayer had become a show, and a demonstration of religious skill to impress others. This show was meant to elevate the Pharisee in the sight of any observers as they spouted longwinded, eloquent prayers. Their goal was to enhance their image as highly spiritual, religious leaders, elevated above the common Jew. Prayer was being used as a platform for pride to

19 Mt 6:5-18
20 Jn 15:5

strut its stuff, instead of the intended purpose of affirming our humble dependence on the Lord.

In contrast to the Pharisees' spiritual show, Jesus calls his followers to pray to the Father in secret, to allow this intimate place of communion to be the backbone of a their prayer lives. Secret prayer requires that you believe that God hears and responds, whereas the "for show" prayer may not include God at all, and may not have any faith involved. The goal of "for show" prayer is image; the goal of secret prayer is relationship.

Today we may not see Pharisees standing on street corners, praying long flowery prayers, but there is an essential principle here that we must apprehend. There is a temptation to forgo a rich personal prayer life in favour of praying in public settings in order to create a show of our superior spirituality. Having a rich personal prayer life doesn't mean we avoid praying in public spaces, but it does mean that our motivation for prayer isn't connected to our public image.

In addition, we can be one that adds drama to our prayers for the sake of impressing our hearers rather than genuinely being moved by a passion that comes from the Holy Spirit. While outwardly the difference between these two may not be apparent, inwardly it is. Each disciple must ask themselves, am I seeking man's approval of my prayer and allowing that to motivate me? Or am I yielding wholeheartedly to God and being moved by his Spirit, whether that leads me to be quiet or passionately demonstrative?

Further, Jesus teaches that private prayer requires intention, it doesn't just happen on its own. This is a vital principle as we seek to apply the Lord's Prayer in our lives, we need to make time and a space, (a closet) for prayer to be expressed. Certainly, you can practice the presence of God and converse with him throughout the day, no matter what you are doing. This is healthy and right. But this can not replace the daily practice of prayer in the secret place. Here we find a private place to meet with God, and we shut the door, eliminating all distractions. This is not a time for multitasking—this type of prayer requires an undivided focus.

The prayer closet is indispensable for completely opening our hearts in every real and raw way that is necessary for full communion with the Lord. Praying the Lord's Prayer successfully requires this type of focus and this kind of private place. So if you haven't already, find a time and a place where you can daily come before the Lord unhindered by distractions.

B. NO EMPTY PHRASES Mt 6:7,8

> *"And when you pray, do not heap up empty phrases as the Gentiles do, for they think that they will be heard for their many words. Do not be like them, for your Father knows what you need before you ask him."*

Jesus has just called his followers to a life of prayer radically different from the Pharisees, now he calls them to also pray in a completely different way from the Gentiles! Jesus' instructions to "not pray empty phrases" found in the English Standard Version are translated from the Greek word *battalogeō.*

Other translations phrase it slightly differently: vain repetitions, meaningless repetition, or babbling like pagans. However, when you look at the Greek root for this word it is even more revealing. The word means: to stammer, to repeat the same thing over and over, to use many idle words. The word was originally derived from the name of a king who was the author of tedious and wordy poems! Jesus is calling his disciples to pray in a completely new way, dismissing what the Pharisees or the Gentiles valued. He's giving his disciples keys to praying powerful, kingdom prayers.

As he does, however, Jesus is not teaching that we shouldn't repeat ourselves in prayer. In Luke he follows up the teaching on the Lord's Prayer with a further exhortation to not just ask, but keep on asking! Repetition isn't the problem, it's disengaged hearts. He is teaching that our words must have sincerity and they must be purposeful. "Vain repetitions", means empty or void of any authentic engagement, like you are praying on auto-pilot, regardless of how formal or spontaneous your prayer is.

You can just as easily pray a spontaneous prophetic prayer that you just don't mean as you can pray the words of an ancient liturgical prayer. The form is not the issue, it's level of earnest, sincere, heart engagement. Do you mean what you are saying? Sadly, the Lord's Prayer is assuredly the prayer that has been prayed the most of any prayer in a "vain repetition" style, forfeiting so much of what could have been gained.

When we pray the Lord's Prayer, we have to discipline ourselves to engage our hearts, to make this prayer our own, to apply it to our situation. Otherwise we are just saying the words and coasting through it without it touching our deepest needs or transforming our hearts.

So whether we stumble into praying publicly in performance mode to enhance our image with others, or allow prayer to become a empty exercise of our lips, thinking that we'll score points with God for logging time, the root issue is the same. Jesus addresses both of these, teaching us to neither pray as the Pharisees or the Gentiles, but as children. He's teaching us that the Father wants our hearts—this is our big take away. Prayer always must be an issue of the heart.

C. WITH TRUST Mt 6:8

"...your Father knows what you need before you ask him."

Prayer in the Old Testament was directed toward the Lord God of Israel; the God of Abraham, Isaac and Jacob. God loved his people, but he was often feared and obeyed in a formal, reverential way rather than known intimately. This was never God's intention. Jesus doesn't reject the revelation of God's holiness and majesty but expands it to reveal that God is also a good, attentive, caring Father. Prayer is to be directed toward the Father, so we can be simple, childlike, and utterly vulnerable without fear.

Jesus is teaching us that we don't have to be anxious about getting every detail of prayer exactly right, using exactly the right words or making sure we don't leave any loopholes for God to misconstrue what we are asking for. We can relax and be ourselves, trusting that our Father not only knows our needs before we ask but knows exactly what we are trying to express, even if we struggle for words. He even hears and understands the prayer of tears, or the prayer of groans too deep for words.

We are not addressing our Judge, we are addressing our Father. He hasn't brought us into a legal courtroom, but welcomed us into his home, seated us at his table. We can rest in his love.

Lists of needs are often shared in prayer meetings, which can be a very helpful way of insuring everyone's able to pray with understanding. But lists can also create problems. When you don't have time to address every need, anxiety can rise, and the temptation is then to treat the prayer list like a "to do" list that demands to be worked through.

Protect your prayer, either in a corporate meeting, or in your personal prayer times, from the temptation of regarding prayer as merely a to-do list of requests. You aren't responsible to pray for every need on your list, Jesus is already doing that. Your role is to lean into him, and trust he has you covered as you pray, directed by and yielded to his Spirit.

D. DAILY Mt 6:11

"Give us this day our daily bread."

Although verse 11 is part of the Lord's Prayer itself, it's an important part of Jesus' "how to" instructions. How we pray it includes: "when do we pray it", and even "how much should we pray it?"

Jesus is pointing us toward praying it daily. He is calling us into a dependence that is equated with our daily necessity for food. This call to dependence, while jarring to our natural orientation of independence is essential for spiritual growth. It's a dependence that is walked out moment by moment, continually leaning on him, abiding in him. The early disciples understood Jesus' teaching to be a very literal invitation to make the Lord's Prayer their daily prayer, and they enthusiastically accepted this invitation, even incorporating the prayer in their three daily hours of prayer.

Those of us who have recommitted to praying the Lord's Prayer are finding, even though we pray it daily, that it never runs dry. It continues to bring us into the Father's heart and align us with his desires, day after day. If we determine to invest our hearts in the prayer, give room for the Spirit to speak and lead, (essentially, just show up with expectation), we will keep encountering him.

E. ADD FASTING Mt 6:16-18

> *"And when you fast, do not look gloomy like the hypocrites, for they disfigure their faces that their fasting may be seen by others. Truly, I say to you, they have received their reward. But when you fast, anoint your head and wash your face, that your fasting may not be seen by others but by your Father who is in secret. And your Father who sees in secret will reward you."*

Fasting has always been added to prayer creating the biblical response to the most desperate needs and serious times of crisis. This duo is looked at as the pull-out-all-stops response to urgent needs. But fasting is not just for special times of acute need. In this passage Jesus teaches that fasting is linked with prayer as a part of the disciplines that draw us closer to God. These are disciplines that we are all called to, so as we seek to grow in prayer, fasting matters. Notice how Jesus begins with "when you fast," rather than, "if you fast." So we can have faith that God will empower us with the grace to add fasting to our lives.

However, fasting has to be done in the right spirit, intentionally choosing weakness and dependence. It increases humility and an awareness of areas in our lives that need to be sanctified. Fasting can break strongholds of sin and bondages of the enemy as we humble ourselves in this way. But in Jesus' day the Pharisees were fasting in an entirely different way, using fasting to bolster their self-righteousness.

So in this passage Jesus uncovers self-righteousness as an often hidden heart issue, one that distorts how we see ourselves. When we are self-righteous we take stock of all our religious works and delight in the (false) perception they give us of having achieved greater righteousness. We measure our lifestyle and compare ourselves with others. With this false perception influencing our self-image, we want others to agree and be impressed with us. This is where fasting for the approval of men comes in. It's for performance, and the root is self-righteousness.

Another way self-righteousness manifests as we fast, is when we approach fasting as if it were a type of a hunger-strike, a way to pressure God into doing something. This absolutely contravenes the biblical meekness, humility, and surrender, that fasting is meant to cultivate. The deceptive root of self-righteousness leads us to think we can gain power to sway God if we do enough extreme religious works.

However, when we combine the Lord's Prayer with our fasting, we are daily uniting with a prayer of surrender, of humility and even repentance. This protects us from self-righteousness or unmasks it if it's already at work. Praying this way helps us to fast in the right spirit, instead of in futility. So praying the Lord's Prayer protects our fasting, and conversely as fasting is added to the Lord's Prayer, the greater spiritual sharpness and dependency it produces marvellously empowers our prayers.

Let's now move over to Luke chapter 11 and consider the verses that surround the Lord's Prayer in this gospel.

F. DISCIPLES Lk 11:1

> *"Now Jesus was praying in a certain place, and when he finished, one of his disciples said to him, 'Lord, teach us to pray, as John taught his disciples.'"*

The first verse of this chapter on prayer opens with the unnamed disciple asking for instruction on prayer and reflecting on how John the Baptist had taught his disciples to pray. This verse emphasizes that those that are truly disciples draw instruction on prayer from their teachers, rather than just making up their own path.

The importance of this simple verse can easily be overlooked, but the truths it contains can set us into a biblical, kingdom, perspective on prayer.

- We are being taught to approach prayer with the humility of a disciple desiring to learn, rather than one who feels his preferred way of prayer is equal in value to what Jesus taught. Even after many years, none of us arrive at becoming prayer professionals. We all need to maintain a teachable, humble heart.
- We are taught that prayer, more than any other activity, is where Jesus' guidance is most acutely needed. This is the only place in the gospels where the disciples directly asked for instruction. Prayer then, is where we should seek to be most closely patterned after Jesus. It's where we should unite with Jesus' desires, carrying his tone, his compassion, and his faith into our intercession.

G. BOLDNESS Lk 11:5-8

"Then Jesus said to them, 'Suppose you have a friend, and you go to him at midnight and say, 'Friend, lend me three loaves of bread; a friend of mine on a journey has come to me, and I have no food to offer him.' And suppose the one inside answers, 'Don't bother me. The door is already locked, and my children and I are in bed. I can't get up and give you anything.' I tell you, even though he will not get up and give you the bread because of friendship, yet because of your shameless audacity he will surely get up and give you as much as you need.'"

After responding to the disciples' request to be taught. The parable of the friend at midnight carries important revelation about the nature of God. Placed in this context, Jesus intended for this parable to give us the confidence to pray boldly to the Father, even approaching God with "shameless audacity".

A unexpected visitor shows up late one night, and the host is caught in a very embarrassing situation—he has nothing to feed his guest! In our North American culture, this would be slightly awkward, but could be easily smoothed over with the promise of a hearty breakfast at a nearby restaurant. Nobody would really mind.

However, in Middle Eastern culture, hospitality is linked with honour and so our poor host was in an excruciating social predicament. His solution was to run to a near-by friend, who would have certainly understood and been sympathetic to his need. But things turn badly, and the friend doesn't want to bother getting out of bed to help.

Jesus is painting a picture that his hearers would have understood was ridiculous. If this man was his friend, and they had a genuine relationship, he would have been more than willing to help. It's preposterous to think that he would leave his friend stuck in this awful situation. But Jesus continues with the story explaining that the friend bangs on the neighbour's door until it is opened, refusing to be denied. He's applying this parable to prayer.

Even though we have a "Friend" in heaven who has all the abundant resources to meet any of our needs and it would be preposterous to think that he would be indifferent to our request, we are encouraged to persist and be bold in our knocking on his door, even if we think he's not responding. The parable is giving us two reasons we can expect to receive, because he is a Good Friend, and because we are unrelenting in our asking.

The phrase "shameless audacity" in the English Standard Version, is translated differently in other Bibles. Translators have used the word boldness, shameless persistence, impudence, and persistence. You get the picture! Jesus is encouraging us to pray boldly, not tentatively or timidly, afraid of bothering God. No, we are to pray with our whole heart asking for the full portion of what we need, for ourselves and any who have "come from afar" to our doors.

Boldness in a strong relationship isn't offensive or out of line. The greater your relationship, the more you know you can ask boldly without jeopardizing it. In this illustration bold asking is modelled and welcomed because of the depth of relationship with the Father that we have if we are in Christ.

Hebrews also teaches us to come boldly before the throne to receive grace and mercy.[21] Although we are never to be disrespectful, we also never have to be fearful, unsure of our standing or acceptance as we pray.

H. PERSEVERANCE Lk 11:9, 10

> *"And I tell you, ask, and it will be given to you; seek, and you will find; knock, and it will be opened to you. For everyone who asks receives, and the one who seeks finds, and to the one who knocks it will be opened."*

Jesus follows on from the parable of the friend at midnight to teach that we should not just pray the Lord's Prayer with boldness, but to keep praying it with great perseverance. The exhortation he gives us in these verses is to ask, seek and knock—to be active and expecting.

The Greek tense for these words is the present active imperative, meaning it could be translated, "ask and keep on asking, seek and keep on seeking, knock and keep on knocking." Jesus is inviting us to stay engaged in prayer, to continue earnestly, until we have our answer. It's this posture of asking, daily asking, with hearts full of faith that brings about the greatest level of breakthrough in prayer.

When we pray the Lord's Prayer there are requests that will never fully be answered in our lifetime, unless Jesus returns. Yet they can be answered *in part* on a daily basis. For example, "Let Your name be hallowed, Your kingdom come, Your will be done on earth as it is in heaven," is a prayer that we see answered in part as the kingdom breaks out in our lives and communities in new or deeper ways, but its fullness will not be realized until the millennial age of the rule of Christ after his

---

21 Heb 4:16

return. It's the "now and not yet" kingdom; the kingdom that is here, but not fully here.

The "ask and keep on asking" posture lives in the reality of the certainty of the coming of the kingdom, full of glory, full of God. It's a posture that scans the horizon with robust faith and notices every big or small way that the kingdom is breaking in and appearing in our field of vision. The "ask and keep asking" posture is energized and optimistic, knowing that every step we take toward the kingdom has an impact. Even our little, weak prayers add to the roar that rises from the earth, crying for Jesus' return and the unfolding of his kingdom in fullness. These prayers are in themselves purposeful and powerful; though alone they are small drops of water, they join with many others in the great torrent of global and historic prayer.

I. HUNGER FOR HOLY SPIRIT Lk 11:13

> *"What father among you, if his son asks for a fish, will instead of a fish give him a serpent; or if he asks for an egg, will give him a scorpion? If you then, who are evil, know how to give good gifts to your children, how much more will the heavenly Father give the Holy Spirit to those who ask him!"*

As we continue reading in Luke 11, we move from the exhortation to ask and keep on asking to teaching on the Good Father. Here Jesus is using another ridiculous, even shocking illustration to memorably drive a point. Jesus teaches that the Father is good, and gives good gifts to his hungry children. He teaches that the Father is not conniving or malicious, he doesn't give what would hurt us when we ask for what we need. He explains that if we know how to give good things to our children (and would never dream of giving them something hurtful), then our Good Father, whose goodness makes ours by comparison seem evil, will all the more give what is good to his children.

It's a teaching about the character of God who is always full of kindness and care toward his children. Yet there is more here than this one truth in the teaching. We also see that God responds to hunger. All of the examples (including the version of this text found in Matthew) are requests for food. An egg, a fish, and some bread[22] are the requests, and Jesus equates them to asking for the Holy Spirit, in need and hunger. We are being invited to ask for the Holy Spirit and expect that the Father will generously give the Spirit, in the same way he would generously give food to a hungry child. In fact there is an expectation that prayer will contain hungry, faith-filled asking for the Spirit.

The other truth we want to glean from this passage, is that with a universally relatable image, Jesus is teaching that prayer is meant to be simple, childlike, and utterly natural. It's meant to be as intimate and relational as a child's daily request for food from their parent.

As we allow the surrounding passages inform the way we approach the Lord's Prayer, it suddenly elevates it out of the place of dry, religious repetition, to the place of dynamic guide for effective, transformative intercession.Our hearts fill with a new found gratitude for this marvellous guide, and a resolve to use it the way Jesus intended.

BY THE SPIRIT

Before we jump into the text of the prayer and unpack how it leads us into the life of God, let's first settle that this is indeed meant to be an outline, a structure for prayer. We are not being restricted to only use the fifty-seven words of the prayer as the way we communicate with the Father. No, it is an outline, and we need the Holy Spirit to fill in the rest.

The Apostle Paul, who would of course have been throughly grounded in the Lord's Prayer, who would have faithfully prayed it and taught it to others, says something surprising in Romans:

"In the same way, the Spirit helps us in our weakness. We do not know what we ought to pray for, but the Spirit himself intercedes for us through wordless groans. And he who searches our hearts knows the mind of the

---

22 Mt 7:9

Spirit, because the Spirit intercedes for God's people in accordance with the will of God." Rom 8:26,27 NIV

Wait a minute! If Jesus has already given us the Lord's Prayer, why would Paul say, "we do not know what we ought to pray for"!? Clearly, there is more to this than just reciting the Lord's Prayer! In fact, Paul is teaching us that the Spirit helps us in our weakness (which he says is lack of revelation or understanding of how to pray).

But the Spirit will go far beyond just directing us towards a topic or prayer need and leaving us to do the rest. He helps us with every aspect of prayer.

He brings us revelation which enlightens and guides our prayer with understanding. This means instead of us having to mentally assess the situation and pray however *we* think would be the best, He reveals how to approach each need. He reveals hidden root issues we wouldn't see on our own, and reveals urgent needs in the exact moments of distress. These are some of the big factors that makes prophetic prayer (or Spirit-led prayer) so effective.

He also brings us the burden of God, so we come alive with passion for the need before us. This can range from a simple sense of stirring, with an awakened concern for a situation, to a deep travailing, a Spirit-led groaning for the need to be met. Either way, Spirit-led, revelatory prayer carries the burden, the heart, and the compassion of God concerning the matter to be prayed for. We're no longer praying about cold, detached facts, but with an impartation from Jesus, the Great High Priest, who is moved with deep compassion.

Paul is not at all calling us to abandon Jesus's teaching on prayer, rather he's amplifying what is taught in the gospels with the understanding that the Lord's Prayer is meant to be a structure that the wind and power of the Spirit will blow through. I often think of a tall ship, beautiful to look at when sitting at dock, but when the sails are unfurled and the wind begins to blow it's more than an admirable piece of craftsmanship, it becomes a mighty vessel moving with grace, power, and speed. It's a vessel that takes you somewhere! In the same way, when the Lord's Prayer is prayed so that the Spirit fills it with the revelation, the burden and the compassion of Jesus, it becomes an extraordinary, exhilarating adventure into fruitful prayer.

We are learning to practice what the Church has long done: praying the Lord's Prayer phrase by phrase, allowing the Holy Spirit to direct our prayers as we expound on each phrase and apply it to our lives and the situations around us. It's fully embracing and yielding to both the Spirit and the Word in the place of prayer. This is authentically praying in Jesus' Name.

With this approach we can pray the Prayer through in just a few minutes if this is all the time we have, or we can allow much more "wind to fill the sails" and can easily take an hour or two to pray without it getting dry or boring.

As we seek to pray under the leading of the Spirit, there will always be phrases or petitions that he highlights and beckons us to pray more deeply. These will take more time and unfold with more revelation. However, the next day it could be an entirely new focus and the Sprit could "blow" on a completely different part of the Prayer.

One day our central focus could be on "Forgive us our sins", spending time praying deeply for a revival of holiness and a love of purity to be granted to the Church. The next day the Spirit could use "Hallowed be Your Name" to direct us into a great burden for the Church in our community to be effective in doing good works which will glorify our Father who is in heaven.[23] A third day could find us spending an extended time praying, under the heading of "Give us this day our daily bread", for a great increase of intimacy with the Spirit (the Bread of His Presence) in our personal lives.

So genuinely welcoming the Holy Spirit into your prayer time is vital. This welcome includes actively listening, responding, and honouring the moving of the Spirit.

Listening - As you pray, tune in to what the Spirit says to you

23 Mt 5:16

through scriptures, impressions, words, or revelatory "ah-ha" moments. This is the root of prophetic, or Spirit-led, prayer. With this approach a great sensitivity as well as an acute spiritual ear can be developed. This hearing gives essential guidance in prayer.

Responding - Hearing alone isn't enough so the next step is responding. Responding involves adjusting the direction of your prayer based on the revelation given, even if it means completely abandoning your planned direction. I often teach people desiring to grow in prayer to "pray from their spirit, rather than their mind", which is another way of expressing this step of responding to the Spirit. It's a helpful way to remind us that we have to be careful not to override our revelatory impressions with our thoughts and opinions of what might be good to pray for.

Honouring - This third aspect of Spirit-led prayer involves not just hearing and responding, but giving enough space in your prayer for the depth and fullness of what God wants to lead you into. It means praying with the depth of the burden that He wants to impart to you, the heights of faith, and staying persistently focused on that petition until the Lord brings you into a place of peace where the unction to pray has lifted. You can practice this in your personal prayer times and also in corporate times, where you together "park" on a particular petition that God is anointing in order to invest more intensity and focus. I train people in this all the time, teaching them to "watch for the oil"—our ministry's term for discerning what the Holy Spirit is anointing—and honouring it.

PRAY IT ALL

There is one more very important point to consider before we look more deeply at the actual Prayer itself. We need to remember that while the two recorded texts that we draw the Lord's Prayer from are slightly different, the sequence is the same. This is really important. Both Mathew (one of the Apostles who walked with Jesus personally) and Luke (who was mentored directly by Paul) record the Prayer with the same opening and general structure. They don't simply list the petitions in a random order, rather, there is agreement that this is the order and flow that Jesus taught. The more we pray it, the easier it is to see the profound wisdom in the sequence of the petitions.

With this in mind, I try to resist the temptation to just cherry-pick whatever petition from the prayer that I feel most stirred about, leaving the rest aside. I also try to ensure I pray the whole prayer through each time I pray it.

As we look more deeply at the various petitions of the prayer it will become apparent why this simple discipline matters so much, but for now, suffice it to say: pray it through in the order Jesus gave it, and pray it all. Pray it daily from your heart, with faith, trust, humility and perseverance. As you do, watch heaven come down.

GROUP DISCUSSION QUESTIONS:

1. What are some of the reasons that Jesus instructed us to "go into your room, shut the door and pray to your Father who is in secret,"? (Mt 6:6)
2. Which of the biblical instructions for how to pray the Lord's Prayer do you find easiest to follow? Which the most challenging?
3. The Holy Spirit helps us as we pray. Is there a specific area you would like more help with?

Chapter Three

OUR FATHER IN HEAVEN

The Prayer that Jesus gave us begins in a way that is universally familiar, even comforting, yet at the same time it radically confronts us with the power of its truth. It opens with a traditional way of addressing God: Our Father. It's an address that brings the reality of our relationship with God front and centre. This reality of God being called Father is delightful for some, but for others it's uncomfortable, even disturbing.

How we relate to God as Father is a dynamic that is fraught with complications, but it cannot be avoided. Jesus was teaching us to pray to his Father; he came both to represent and reconcile us with his Father. Yet, sadly, for many this opening is a stumbling block. It conjures up an image of a distant, stern, Victorian-era father, who tolerates his children until they mature; or an image of a divine ruler sitting on his throne in heaven, putting up with us and all our shortcomings, while full of disappointment and disapproval. We call him Father because that's his title, not because it expresses the bond and nature of our relationship.

For others, even the word Father is a source of pain, confusion, or anger, as our past experiences with our earthly fathers have fallen short. Many of these relationships have been deeply broken, so much that even this word, "Father" reawakens feelings of wounding from abandonment, abuse or neglect. Jesus knew all of this when He gave us this prayer. Could it be that calling us to pray to the Father is an act of love, gently lifting the bandages that cover our wounded hearts, cleansing and pouring out healing as many times as we need? It also begins to redeem the concept of Father as we discover him to be faithful, infinitely loving, attentive and absolutely safe.

However, for the Jewish disciples who were being instructed in how to pray, the concept of calling God, "Father" was shocking for an entirely different set of reasons.

Throughout the Old Covenant God was revealed as the Almighty, the Holy One, the Creator, the Lord God of Israel, but rarely as Father. When he was, it was generally that the word "Father" was used to express that he was the source of our life as our Creator. But Jesus came to reveal the Father, and a part of that revelation was showing us what perfect relationship with the Father looked like. He modelled a relationship of love, trust, communion, complete dependence, obedience, surrender, delight, and restful abiding. His relationship with the Father was the foremost feature of his life, right from our first glimpse of him at the young age of twelve, where he was surprised that Mary and Joseph didn't automatically know he would be "in [his] Father's house" when they realized he was missing.[24] Consider also, all the language Jesus used to express both deep relationship with the Father and his confident identity as the Son. This was how Jesus spoke when he taught, with language that seemed blasphemous to the religious hearers. But it wasn't a one-sided relationship; the Father continually endorsed and validated Jesus' Sonship.

The Father celebrated Jesus' birth with an angelic choir and he poured out his Spirit upon Christ without measure, beginning at his baptism where the Holy Spirit descended in the form of a dove. The Father publicly announced his pleasure and relationship with Jesus, his audible voice declaring "This is my Beloved Son, with whom I am well

---

24 Lk 2:49

pleased".[25] Again on the Mount of Transfiguration his audible voice declared "This is my Son, my Chosen One, listen to him!".[26] Finally, before the cross when Jesus prayed that the Father would be glorified, God responded from heaven with a final statement over Jesus' life: "I have glorified it, and I will glorify it again," (meaning that he has glorified his name through the life Jesus led, and was now about to glorify it through Jesus' death and resurrection).[27]

The Father also endorsed all that Jesus taught (including his teaching on the nature of his relationship with the Father), by releasing though him unprecedented signs and wonders, healings and miracles. There was a supernatural presence and dimension to all Jesus taught and did to such a degree that people knew He just had to say a word and a child, not even present, would be healed or delivered from demonic torment. Others knew that if they simply touched him (or even the hem of his clothing), their crippling needs would be met.

But the greatest and most powerful endorsement and validation of the Son by the Father, was the resurrection. The Jewish religious leaders, Roman authorities, and even the Jewish people all weighed Jesus in the balance and decided he was not the Son of God he claimed to be. They declared him to be a fraud.[28] But the Father had the final word and he raised Jesus from the dead into power and glory, affirming for those in all of history to know for certain, that this is The Beloved Son, in whom he is forever well pleased.

Jesus had come to reveal the Father. He did it perfectly and the Father spectacularly endorsed him.

This revelation Jesus brought us was an invitation into relationship, an invitation extended to a world of orphans to be adopted by a perfect Father. Christ lived out and displayed his relationship with the Father before us, and then invited us into it, a relationship full of fellowship,

---

25 Mt 3:17
26 Lk 9:35
27 Jn 12:28
28 Mt 27:63

tenderness and care, able to touch, and heal, and satisfy the deepest longings of a human heart.

Therefore, when Jesus instructs us to pray, "Our Father...," he is drawing us into his relationship with his Father. It's as if he is standing as our older brother, putting his arm around our shoulder, and leading us into his beautiful, and powerful union with his Father by leading us in this prayer.

This was a shocking new way of relating to God, so different than what the Jewish disciples had been accustomed to. Jesus changed everything. This revelation, and the door it opened into relationship with the Father so impacted the early disciples, that the New Testament is full of language speaking of God as Father, even using the tender, intimate term of Abba. This was a massive, revolutionary paradigm shift.

Embracing the revelation of God as our Father is the door that we walk through to enter into the power of this prayer. It's also the over-arching relational reality that colours how we pray all the petitions of the Prayer. Whether we pray for forgiveness, or the provision of daily bread, we do so as children addressing our Father. This shifts the whole prayer into exhilarating faith as we remember Jesus' words to us, spoken in the context of the teaching on the Lord's Prayer, "... if you, being evil know how to give good gifts to your children—HOW MUCH MORE...".[29]

With all this in mind, let's look deeper at the words "Our Father who is in heaven" and explore some of the profound revelations that we can pray through in these first few words of the Prayer. The goal at this point is to whet your appetite and open your heart to the breadth and depth of how it can be prayed, so that you dive in and allow the Holy Spirit to lead you into praying it in life-giving ways.

As we pray, let's ponder every word, paying attention to what the Holy Spirit is revealing and how He is using all of this to activate us

---

29 Lk 11:13

in prayer. Suddenly, the prayer becomes rich with revelation and the revelation leads us into intercession. It begins with "Our".

OUR

Right at the outset we are declaring we are a part of a family, a people, a community. We are standing together. We belong to the Father and to each other. Once were not a people, but now we have become the people of God.[30] Because of this, we are not alone, and as we pray, we are affirming our union with Christ and the whole Church. Immediately, any sense of isolation or loneliness we've been experiencing gives way to the reality of the magnitude of the company we are joined to in Christ. A massive, eternal family.

We are a part of a global community, united as siblings with believers from almost every nation, language, and people group. Imagine for a moment the cry of "Our Father" rising from all over the globe, all day and all night, from hundreds of millions of voices. We are joining this throng.

We are also united as a family with those that have gone before us. These ones passed away leaving behind them godly prayers based on the Lord's Prayer that were not fully answered. Our prayers pick up their cause, for we are of the same heart, awakened to the same longings. Our prayer is not a lone voice crying in the wilderness, but one joined into the glorious roar of global, historic intercession that continues to get louder and stronger.

As we open the prayer with, "Our," and the reality of this unity rushes in, it not only breaks our sense of loneliness and isolation, but it also begins to displace the modern, Western mindset of individualism, self-determination, and self-actualization. This is a mindset so contrary to the biblical perspective, yet still unrelentingly seeps into our thinking, unless we intentionally stand guard. Right at the outset, Jesus is making it clear that relationship with God involves "we" not just "me".

---

30 1 Pt 2:10

Yes, each of us needs a personal relationship with the Lord, but the independence we are so familiar with in our culture pushes this need to an extreme. Full-throttled individualism leads to the idolatry of self and bears the fruit of profound loneliness, and a stunted relationship with God.

While this is a reminder that we are not alone in a "Jesus and me" independent and isolated bubble, it is also a reminder to not just pray for ourselves. This means when we pray "Our" there is a call to intercede for more than just our personal needs and difficulties. We are to bear one another's burdens and carry each other in genuine concern. Jesus modelled this as he faced the cross, the most intense and horrific ordeal imaginable, yet even still, in the Garden of Gethsemane, he prayed for us. Indeed, two thirds of Jesus' prayer recorded in John 17 is for the Church—for you and I—even though the cross was just hours away.

Beginning with "Our" puts all this in perspective.

FATHER

As I mentioned, the opening addresses God as Father, not just as a title, but as a glorious revelation and a declaration of relationship. Because we are *instructed* to pray this way, it conveys his heart towards us, his availability, the adoption and identity he gives us.

There is no human fathering that has ever surpassed the love and goodness that our Heavenly Father fathers us with. We are completely known in all our immaturity, sin and weakness—yet absolutely loved to our core. We don't have to hide anything, earn access, or measure up to any standard to come to him. Jesus has done it all. Jesus has given to us credit for all the loving, wise, holy and brave ways he walked, the goodness and grace that he spoke with and the fruitfulness of his life. This is what it means to be clothed in Christ's righteousness. It's not just being washed of sin, but it's getting credit for everything Jesus did, thought, prayed and believed so perfectly. This leaves us with nothing to prove, to earn or to be ashamed of. We come boldly to the Father in

Christ, enjoying his declaration of pleasure over us (the very same as He declared over Jesus) as He receives us into his throne room. He is not embarrassed to be seen with us, he enjoys being our Father. He is always for us and we will always be his delight.

When we consider that we are adopted, but Jesus is the begotten Son of God, it's possible for us, in our earthly brokenness and distortions to overlay *our* earthly perspective of adoption into this relationship. For some of us, this concept might communicate a second-rate child, a child that is "on probation" or a child that is included in a family as long as they don't require anything more than a casual investment. These ideas are completely foreign to what the gospel teaches about adoption. The fact that we are adopted means that the Father went out of his way to seek us out, redeem us through his Son's death and has chosen us to be in eternal covenant with him. He perfectly loves us as he loves Jesus and gives us all the access, rights and duties of a member of his family. Our Father knew what he was getting into when he adopted us; no area of our life in need of redemption, sanctification, healing, and maturing is a surprise to him. None of that caused him to hesitate in his decision to adopt us. There is absolute security in our adoption; we will never be discarded or disinherited.

This reality in itself should be life changing for us and cause worship and thanks to pour from our hearts. Many people, when re-introduced to the Lord's Prayer, find that they spend the first few months camped on these first two words, letting "Our Father", and all that that these words mean, wash over their hearts. These times often turn to repenting for misconceptions and distortions of the Father, being healed and set free into brand new, invigorated fellowship with him.

Because we address him as our Father, when we begin to press into a fuller revelation of what this means, all the fear, hesitancy, distance and formality is removed from our prayer. But it doesn't mean that we shift into a casual or disrespectful familiarity as we come near to him. We still need to be very aware that he is God Almighty. We will look more deeply at this in later chapters, but at this point it's enough to say that "Our Father" is both a declaration of intimacy and respect.

Let's now spend some time considering what a child could receive from their father, in the most optimal and healthy relationship conceivable.[31]

SECURITY

In a healthy father-child relationship, the child is secure to the core of their heart. They are not anxious about the future, their personal safety, or the nature of their relationship with their father changing. They can be at rest and as a result, joy, peace, confidence and optimism flow from their life. They never have to anxiously check to see if their father is still around or following through with his promises; they completely take this for granted. This gives the child the emotional capacity to create, to dream, to cultivate vision and to generously pour into others. It builds courage in them.

In addition, this child is secure in knowing that their father will protect them, that he's able to do so and committed to watch over their lives to guard them emotionally, physically, spiritually and in many other ways. There are times that a father allows a child to struggle a bit, to take risks, to sacrifice, even to get hurt so that they can grow into maturity, but there is always a limit to how much a good father allows before he steps in and rescues his child.

But even though earthly fathers may excel at building security into the lives of their children, they still pale in comparison with the skill and goodness of our Heavenly Father.

ACCEPTANCE

---

31 While we are going to focus specifically on fathers, most of these points could easily apply to mothers as well. Not mentioning mothers in each point, is for the sake of simplicity and clarity, and not meant to be interpreted as discounting, in any way their critical role in a child's life.

No matter how weak a child is or what they struggle with, a healthy father unconditionally accepts and covers his child where they fail or fall short. There is no need for the child to better themselves before he accepts them, the father knows about these weakest areas and embraces the child regardless. Their love and acceptance is free of judgments, conditions, the need to perform or achieve. Love and acceptance are never withheld as a motivator to change behaviour.

All the more, our Heavenly Father sees every deep place of sin, brokenness and darkness in our lives and extends grace to cover them all. He is infinitely patient as we repeatedly stumble into the same selfish habits. Our welcome into his presence and into his heart is never in jeopardy. His expectations of us are perfectly matched with both our capacity and his empowerment, so we never have to live trapped under a cloud of disappointment.

ACCESS

Children have the unique privilege of having access to their fathers whenever they need them. The father could be a king, a surgeon, a judge, the CEO of a major corporation, or a famous celebrity, but the child has privileged access.

When we consider our Heavenly Father, this unfettered access becomes even more profound. He always has time for us, always is listening when we cry out to him, always understands what we mean when we are fumbling for words. We, as his children, have the most privileged place of access of all. Angels come when they are summoned; we come to him whenever we desire.

DISCIPLINE

Hebrews teaches us that discipline is a sign of a true father-child relationship, and it is a mark of the investment of a father into his true children.[32]

---

32 Heb 12:5-11

While most of us have had less-than-optimal discipline from our fathers, the image that the writer of Hebrews gives us of the Father's discipline is that it is for our training and it produces righteousness (integrity and right-living) in our lives.

Healthy, godly discipline doesn't leave scars of trauma, fear, or confusion. It is a consistent enforcing and reminding the child of healthy, holy, boundaries, training the child to self-regulate their behaviour so eventually, external discipline isn't needed. It is a costly investment into the child, one that comes from a heart of love.

Healthy fathers care deeply about their children's discipline so that their daughters and sons are godly in character and set up for success in all of their endeavours.

PROVISION

Today, parenting is considerably more complicated than in previous generations. In my childhood, growing up in the 60s, the expectation was that parents provided their children with food, clothing, housing, medical care when needed and sometimes help toward a post-secondary education. Beyond that, children were pretty much on their own. The concept of being aware of and seeking to provide for the needs of a child's heart was quite foreign. Needs like encouragement, affirmation, community, or opportunities to explore special talents, were not generally considered to be the primary responsibility of a parent.

While it's unrealistic to expect earthly parents to be able to meet every need, our Heavenly Father is more than able and absolutely willing to do so. All of our physical and spiritual needs are met by him, but we can also look to him for the authentic needs of our hearts.

His provision is completely without reproach. It's generous, wise, abundant and right on time. Even when we can't figure out what we need, he knows. He is a profoundly good Father in motivation, but also in skill.

INSTRUCTION

Fathering has always included some aspects of instructing. A father teaches his children and is a ready resource for knowledge and wisdom.

In biblical days this was a particularly central aspect of the father-son relationship, as fathers were expected to apprentice their sons, teaching them the family trade or profession. Sons didn't go to a career fair to explore vocational direction; they grew up helping their fathers, expecting to carry on in the family business or trade.

Of course, this has a beautiful application to us, regardless of being male or female, as the Father's instruction for life and blessing is readily available to us. Then even beyond this, we are all welcomed into the "apprenticeship program" where we are instructed and discipled to become more and more like Christ. With the empowering of the Father's instruction we are sent out to serve in the "family mission" where we take up his passion to see the gospel of Jesus transform our needy world.

GUIDANCE

Similar to instruction, fathers guide their children in making life decisions. The father's age and experience give perspective and wisdom to his children, as he is able to guide them away from pitfalls and into choices that allow them to flourish. Even adult children will seek out the counsel of wise parents before making any significant decisions. How much more will our Heavenly Father have wisdom and perspective to guide us into paths of life and calling.

AFFIRMATION

There may not be many more powerful words than the words of affirmation from a parent to a child. Children look to their fathers for unqualified affirmation, signs that the fathers are genuinely celebrating who they are and what they've done. When this need is not fulfilled we see children subconsciously driven all their days to please their fathers, even after they've passed away.

A healthy father pours a steady flow of authentic, verbal, even public affirmation into their children. Along with affirmation, it is the continual encouragement that deeply strengthens hearts and builds endurance into children.

Our Heavenly Father created your heart to need these life-giving words, so it's never off-limits to ask him to speak them over you. However, it is our role to receive them as truth. For those that haven't been accustomed to the Father's affirmation, it can be very uncomfortable initially, until we train ourselves to simply receive, rather than deflecting or subtly rejecting his affirmation. There are many ways this can come to us: through the voice of others, scripture or the Lord speaking to us directly.

SUPPORT

Whenever a child is facing a challenge, the support of their parents can be the game-changer. At its core, support is the parent simply being there, being present with them so they never face the challenge alone. It's facing the challenge with them, looking for ways to help them succeed and overcome the difficulties and setbacks, it's cheering them on. It's a statement of, "I believe in you," and, "your success matters to me."

The opposite of this support is abandonment, which drains resolve, strength and courage from a child. Our Father has pledged to never leave us or forsake us. This doesn't just mean he'll be in the general vicinity, like being within earshot, but intimately present, because his Spirit is within us. He is present in everything: in our times of doubt, in times of anger, in times of despair and lostness. Nothing that we walk through is faced alone.

A NAME

Traditionally, one of the most important things that a father gives to his child is the family name. It brings clarity to identity and communicates to the outside world the nature of the relationship, along with all the rights and privileges it bestows. Having your father's name means that everyone knows his resources and authority can be mobilized to support you whenever needed.

Carrying your father's name can also involve carrying his reputation and honour so that your life and decisions can either reflect well or badly on this name. In the same way we carry our Heavenly Father's name and his reputation and honour is either increased or diminished by how we live. He has entrusted us with a great responsibility by giving us his name. The expectation is that a father will influence by modelling values, behaviour and character for his children and thus the children's behaviour and character is a commentary on the parenting and character of the parent.

This is why in Matthew 5:14-16, Jesus calls his disciples to do good works in their community. Because they represent the Father as sons, their good works bring him glory and reveal his love and mercy to the world.

A PLACE

Being given a place involves fathers making a way for their children to have a significant, meaningful role where they can truly flourish. It could involve funding education or using family contacts to introduce them to opportunities, all for the sake of the child coming into their full potential and in a sense, their true calling.

But with younger children, it's not as much about a successful launch into a career but drawing them into the family's activities and work that gives them significance. Even at a young age, children contribute to their family. In a healthy family, no child is overlooked; all have ways to add to the life and joy of the family, with their gifts and talents finding room and encouragement to develop.

Every child has a place, a place that only they can fill, a place of significance.

INHERITANCE

Receiving an inheritance from an earthly parent is a mixed blessing, as it involves the loss of a parent, but the gain of unearned assets. It's a gift, a trust, a final legacy to the child who in most cases, did nothing for it; it's simply received because of who they are.

However, in terms of our Heavenly Father, we receive an inheritance without the grief of having been orphaned. Where it is the same however, is that it is entirely unmerited, unearned and it comes to us solely by virtue of our sonship or daughterhood. We are his. All our gain is based on relationship and the magnitude of the inheritance we have in Christ is stunning.

As we consider these varied aspects of what children can receive by being fathered, it turns us toward our Heavenly Father with an awareness of how we might need to be fathered by him in a deeper way. He is the ultimate father, the only one who can bring us all of these blessings we long for in their fullest and purest form. He just waits for us to ask. Praying, "Our Father," can begin a journey of healing and open up relationship with God in wonderful new ways.

SIBLINGS

The growing relationship we have with our Heavenly Father is personal, deep and unique, but being in relationship with him means that we have also been brought into his family: a huge, glorious, diverse family. Our spiritual brothers and sisters are genuinely that; they *are* brothers and sisters and will be eternally. So how we interact with them matters very much to our Father.

Every healthy parent loves their children and longs for them to love one another other, walking in unity and close-knit relationship. Jesus' prayer in John 17 and his continual instructions to his disciples to love and serve each other display the Father's heart in this. Remember the Son is the exact representation of the Father, and if we have seen the Son, we have seen the Father.[33] This means that whatever Jesus is passionate about and committed to reveals the Father's passion and commitment. The unity of the Church is very high on this list. As we pray the Lord's Prayer, the Holy Spirit will often lead us in intercession for unity as we consider that we, the Body of Christ, are one family and have one Father.

This opens up opportunity for repentance if we have not aligned with the Father's heart for unity in his family. Perhaps we have walked in spiritual pride, division, or elitism; or perhaps our church or denomination has stumbled in this way. We cannot look down on another or treat them like they are less important to the Father than we are. There is no room in the family of God for these kinds of attitudes. As we humbly repent and intercede for unity, the Lord will do great things to move upon hearts, bring reconciliation and build friendships. This is a prayer He loves to answer.

At times the issue is not broken relationships or division, but the need we are led to in prayer is to remember our brothers and sisters who are suffering. They need their spiritual family to carry them in prayer as they are living under persecution, extreme poverty or oppression of different kinds. Many Christians, our brothers and sisters, are right now in prison because of their faith, others have been orphaned or lost a spouse because they would not deny Christ. Let us pray for these ones.

Finally, as we conclude our thoughts about the dynamics of spiritual family, we all intuitively know that in a healthy family, there is no favouritism. Every child is equally treasured and given opportunity to thrive. This is also true in our heavenly family and it's a glorious revelation that may bring adjustment to how we see ourselves or how we treat each other. We've already reflected on the importance of being washed from spiritual pride, but we also need to remember that there is

33 Heb 1:3, Jn 14:9

no special access given to high-profile Christians. We have no less value or access than the most amazing hero of the faith or modern-day Christian celebrity. Every child of God has full access to the Father through Christ and can come as near as we desire.

Paul, writing in Galatians 3:26-28, teaches us that in Christ there is no privileged group or upper class. Our ethnicity, gender or social strata are all immaterial when we come to the Father. We truly stand on equal ground at the foot of the cross.

GIVER OF LIFE

Our Father is our source of life, our Creator. He is the one who formed us in our mothers' wombs and determined our uniqueness. He made us in his image. It is important that we accept how He made us and seek to dedicate all our skills, efforts and natural talents to his glory. This perspective flies in the face of the modern trend towards self-rejection and loathing as well as the opposite trend of self-glorification and narcissism. Neither perspective is founded on biblical truth and both lead to brokenness. Agreeing with the truth of God as our Creator who declared "it is good" over all that He made brings us into a place of health and peace.[34] This may be an area where we need to invest more prayer, asking the Lord to heal us and lead us into a full acceptance of who we are. It could also be a powerful place for intercession to rise in our hearts for those who struggle with their self-image.

When considering God as our source of life and the source of all life, it's natural to intercede over areas of barrenness or where things seem to have died in our lives, families, churches or communities. The life the Father releases is abundant, reproducing and very good. Even if we have walked through seasons of death in the dealings and sanctifying purposes of God, we can seek him for resurrection life to burst forth and bring glory to his name.

34 Gen 1:31

IN HEAVEN

Recognizing that our Father is in heaven sets us up to pray in faith. He is high above the chaos and tribulation of this world; he sees all, rules over all. He is omnipotent, omniscient, omnipresent and sovereign. Yet he is intimately involved in our lives, even as he sits enthroned in majestic splendour.

The Hebrews considered "in the heavens" to refer to existing in the spiritual atmosphere, rather than in a distant location (perhaps somewhere past Jupiter), so being "in the heavens" doesn't mean that the Father's not perfectly present in our lives.

David declares that, *"He who sits in the heavens laughs"* in Psalms 2:4; Isaiah reveals that *"It is he who sits above the circle of the earth, and its inhabitants are like grasshoppers; who stretches out the heavens like a curtain, and spreads them like a tent to dwell in; who brings princes to nothing, and makes the rulers of the earth as emptiness."*[35] This perspective of the Lord being securely and eternally established as the Ruler of Heaven and Earth brings peace and comfort to our hearts in times of turmoil. While this thought may not be new, allowing the power of its truth to impact us brings us into a more biblical posture of peace, humility and faith.

It also speaks to the wisdom of the Father's will, derived from his perspective from "high above" and his perspective of seeing all, knowing all. From this vantage point God's plans for humanity and for each of our lives are fully informed, flowing from his profound goodness. When we are in the throes of darkness, pain or suffering, God's sovereignty may seem cold and distant, but these difficult times give us an opportunity to trust his character all the more and encounter deeper places of communion with Jesus.

Finally, recognizing that He is in the heavens and so awesome in power, splendour and glory helps us be positioned appropriately in a

---

35 Isa 40:22,23

posture of humility which leads us right into praying that his great name would be hallowed—the next phrase and first petition of the prayer.

APPLYING IT IN PRAYER

The Lord's Prayer is meant to be prayed personally, in a devotional way that is applied to our own relationship with Jesus, but it's also meant to be prayed for others in intercession. Let's consider different ways this first phrase might stir us to prayer.

These are a few illustrations of the ways the words, "Our Father" could launch you into prayer. Keep in mind however, that there are countless ways the Spirit could lead you as you pray these two beautiful words, so these suggestions are merely to get you started.

- Bring us to a greater revelation of sonship
- Deliver us from all anxiety and worry for our needs to be provided and lead us into childlike trust
- Father us in areas where we have been insecure
- Forgive us for self-rejection or self-glorification; heal us
- Help us to exhibit our heavenly "family traits"; make us like you Father, we want it to be obvious to everyone that we are your children
- Teach us to lay our lives down for each other like true brothers and sisters
- Pour out the revelation of your Father-heart on our community, soften hearts to hear the gospel
- Establish us deeply in your love
- Heal areas where we have felt like orphans, or where past experiences distorted our perceptions of you, Father
- Forgive us for believing lies and the enemy's accusations against you Father

- Lead us away from all works or performance, rooted in seeking to win your approval
- Bring reconciliation and restore unity where there has been division
- Lead the global Body of Christ into greater, deeper, unity—let us be one
- Forgive us for envy, jealousy, pride, or competing with our spiritual brothers and sisters
- May I be a better father, mother, sister, son, etc…; may our natural families be more like what you model for family. Bring health and life to our families
- Increase faith in the Church for all you will do as we become awakened to the depth of your heart toward your children
- May fresh encounters of the Father's love and good intentions for us activate much more asking; may all kinds of prayer burst forth
- Restore those who have wandered away as prodigals
- Provide and care for the persecuted Church; we remember our brothers and sisters

SCRIPTURES TO MEDITATE ON

- This is My Beloved Son—Mt 3:17
- This is My Son, hear him—Lk 9:35
- Every good and perfect gift—Jas 1:17
- Spirit of Sonship—Rom 8:15-17, Gal 4:6
- Brothers and sisters—Heb 2:10-12
- Loved and disciplined—Heb 12:5-11
- Dependent on Father—Jn 5:20, 21

- I do nothing independently—Jn 8:28
- Adopted—Eph 1:5,6
- Children of God—1Jn 3:1-3
- Love of the Father—Jn 3:16,17
- Rooted and grounded—Eph 3:14-19
- Nothing will separate us—Rom 8:31-39
- Inheritance of saints—Col 1:12,13
- Highly valued—Mt 10:29, 30
- Prodigals return—Lk 15:18, 21
- I could call upon My Father—Mt 26:53
- Submitted to the Father—Mk 14:36, Lu 23:46

GROUP DISCUSSION QUESTIONS:

1. In what areas of your relationship with God do you need to experience more of his fathering?
2. How does it feel for you to pray, "Our Father"?
3. Does considering that God being our father makes all Christians siblings change the way you view others, or the way you pray?

Chapter Four

HALLOWED BE YOUR NAME

Once we have stepped into the Lord's Prayer with the opening address of "Our Father" we begin a journey through a series of petitions which lead us closer to the Lord, to his will and to becoming more like him. This is the daily journey of a disciple and as it becomes a familiar, well-trodden path, instead of growing stale, the revelation and encounter keeps getting richer and fuller.

The prayer is short enough to be easily memorized and prayed in twenty seconds, but broad enough to encompass every imaginable need. It keeps us tethered to God's heart, so we don't wander off in prayer, giving time and energy to things that are not biblical. When we pray this way, we are focused on the roots of the issues rather than flailing around trying to chop off all the shoots and branches, the symptoms of the problems. Jesus always works from the heart out and the Lord's Prayer functions this way as well. It changes our heart and focuses our intercession on the heart of the matter as we pray for ourselves and others.

IN JESUS' NAME

Jesus also reveals his heart in a deep way through this prayer; here he discloses many of his values and priorities. These values enable us to line up with what matters to him, in order to pray effectively in his name. We understand that praying in Jesus' name involves praying as if we were an agent for Jesus, as one who is interceding for the very thing that he would intercede for; it's prayer that's perfectly aligned with the heart and intention of the Father. It's following the path of Jesus' perfect submission to the Father's will, not just trying to ramp up the impact of our prayer by name-dropping ("In Jesus' name") as we close!

> *John 13:14-15 "Whatever you ask in my name, this I will do, that the Father may be glorified in the Son. If you ask me anything in my name, I will do it."*

When we pray the Lord's Prayer, from our heart, we are praying in Jesus' name. This is why the answers to prayer skyrocket when we begin to use the Lord's Prayer as the core of our prayer life!

More deeply adopting his values and priorities as our own enables us to grow even more in praying in Jesus' name. Here in the Lord's Prayer, not only are many of Jesus' priorities revealed, they are set in order. What matters most to him? We can learn this from the Lord's Prayer. The first three petitions, that the Father's name would be honoured (or hallowed), that his kingdom would come and that his will would be done, all reveal Jesus' commitment to the first and greatest commandment.[36] He didn't just give it, he lived it! These first three petitions are all focused on the Father and come out of the Son's love and surrender to him. It is a true walking out of the commandment to "Love the Lord your God with all your heart, soul, mind and strength".

When we pray through these first three petitions each day, we can expect to experience a change in heart and perspective. We are pulled into seeking the Lord and his righteousness as our greatest priority, finding all the "other things" are easily and naturally added to us.[37]

Let's now look deeper at the first petition: "Hallowed be your name".

---

36 Mt 22:38
37 Mt 6:33

HALLOWED BE

What does this actually mean? How do we pray this earnestly, with hearts full of faith if we're unclear what we are asking for? The word "hallowed" is rarely used in our modern vernacular and sounds to our ears like an ancient and religious word. So how do use effectively it in prayer?

The essence of hallowed is to be made holy, or to be revered as holy. This creates another problem, for how do you *make* the name of God holy, when he is *already* utterly holy and even the source of all holiness? Good question!

This petition is a cry for the name of God to be treated as holy; to be "made holy" on earth in the same way it's revered, honoured and treated as holy in heaven. In addition, because the name represents the person, we are asking that God himself would be honoured. There is a massive gap between how the Lord is honoured in heaven and how He is honoured on earth. This is the gap we stand in as we pray.

In heaven, the name of God and God himself, is perfectly and absolutely revered, worshiped, adored and exalted. Jesus brought this reality to earth, as he brought the revelation of the Father and then modelled the right response to that revelation. Our prayer is may it be on earth, as it is in heaven.

Setting this petition first reveals Jesus' fiercest passion and desire: that the Father's name would be hallowed, that the Father would be known and hallowed on earth. This was, and is, the fiery zeal at the centre of the Son's mission and identity, as it is to be ours. It's a prayer that poured out of Jesus' heart in other settings, recorded in John's gospel: Jn 12:28, 13:31, 17:1, 4-5. So, we can see this was a prayer always near the surface in Jesus' life.

WORSHIP

We can also approach this petition as a declaration of worship (Holy is your Name!) and spend much time in prayer exalting the Lord. This is absolutely fitting and the more we praise, the more we find reasons to praise!

We can also pray for true, worthy worship to flow from our lives. When we worship in a halfhearted, disengaged and distracted way (as we so often are tempted to do), is God honoured in a similar way to how he's being honoured in heaven? When we consider the majesty, glory and love of God, the stunning sacrifice of the Son and the transforming power of the Spirit, shouldn't our worship be a response of adoring intensity? How could we hold back? Sadly, we often wring out a "sacrifice of praise," acting as if we are doing God a favour.

Another oft missing component to our worship is the substance of faith. We may worship with a lack of intensity and conviction when we are uncertain if we actually believe what we are saying. Doubt-riddled worship is so different than the glory of heavenly worship. This is very much a prayer need: that each of us would be so thoroughly convinced of who Jesus is, that worship would naturally, unwaveringly, pour out of our lives.

Praying, "Hallowed be your name" could become a cry for our lives to be full of God-honouring worship, regardless of our personal situation. It could also be a cry of intercession, that worship would erupt in our corporate gatherings that goes far beyond just enjoying the music or the comforting familiarity of a ritual. Rather, worship which is so glorious, it confirms to onlookers that there is something transcendent and real happening in our midst, that God himself is with us.

LIFESTYLE

In Romans 12, the apostle Paul teaches us to present our bodies as a living sacrifice, holy and acceptable to God, which is our spiritual worship.[38] Offering a sacrifice was the primary way the Jews worshiped, so this passage is calling us to not just offer our Sunday praise, but to offer our bodies (lifestyle) as if they were laid on the altar and fully devoted to him.

---

38 Rom 12:1

As we pray "Hallowed be your name", there is a need to pray that God would be fully hallowed: honoured and glorified in every area of our lives. Here our intercession becomes a prayer to receive the power to display him as holy through our lifestyles.

If the way we live is out of sync with the teaching and values of Jesus, how can the Father be glorified in our lives? Praying this prayer can take us into a time for the Lord to reveal to us where changes might need to be made, whether subtle or sweeping, with wide-ranging ramifications. It could also be that we just need to be more self-aware because we've been oblivious that our actions or attitudes have been bringing dishonour instead of glory to the Father.

The problem could also be much more blatant, where our lives (or church communities) are dishonouring God through hypocrisy, pride or other roots of sin. Whenever we walk in contradiction and our words don't match our walk, our actions always speak loudest. Those hypocritical actions or even just undisciplined and immature actions, could be sabotaging our witness or testimony. Father, show us these things so that we could turn from them!

While living a holy life is essential, there is another vital way the Father gains glory from our lifestyle. Jesus led a life full of the power of the Spirit. He healed the sick, received divine revelation and words of knowledge, cast out demons, took authority over the wind and waves and multiplied food. He walked supernaturally and his lifestyle confirmed his message. For us, being filled with the Spirit and his supernatural power will also result in glory, praise and honour going to the Father. Let's make this a part of what we ask for.

Consider for a moment the glory that can come to God when his people demonstrate the character of Jesus, even under pressure. Consider how his reputation and fame can increase as his supernatural power is a daily part of our lifestyle.

NOT OUR NAME

While we are focusing on this petition and the ways we can ask for the Lord's name to be honoured and glorified, if we were to be honest, we might admit that there are times when we'd rather like a measure of that honour.

At times we struggle with a longing for our names to be noticed and honoured for at least some of the praise and accolades to be pointed in our direction. This desire can come from two places: a deep heart-need for affirmation (which can only be satisfied and healed by the Father's love) or from a prideful ego. We crave to be the centre of attention. As we pray this part of the Lord's Prayer, it presents a great opportunity to take stock, to ask him to show us if we are seeking to redirect honour to ourselves. If we are, why? Is there a need for emotional healing in our life or has our self-centeredness been exposed? Are we self-promoting? When we give a testimony, does it leave the hearers more impressed with us or with Jesus? Are we actually boasting in ourselves rather than giving glory to the Lord? It's never wise to seek to rob the Lord of the glory due him, so praying this prayer gives us an opportunity to see this human inclination brought to the cross in repentance.

FEAR OF THE LORD

The petition that longs for God's name to be hallowed is also a petition for the fear of the Lord to grace our lives and the Church. The fear of the Lord is profoundly precious, as it is what enables us to truly revere the name of the Lord. Without it we remain spiritually dull and the awe of God is veiled to us.

The fear of the Lord is not a popular concept in our times, but it is a thoroughly biblical one; the Holy Spirit is called the Spirit of the Fear of the Lord in Isaiah 11.[39] When the fear of the Lord rests on our lives we are careful to live in a way that he would approve. It's not that

39 Isa 11:2

we walk on eggshells but rather that we are aware that he is with us and his presence is holy. This changes our response when tempted to careless words, indulgent behaviour or secret areas of compromise.

The fear of the Lord wonderfully encounters our lives with his holy presence, but can also have a profound impact on a church or even our society. Praying for the fear of the Lord to be poured out in the Church or in our nation is asking the Father to release that same holy presence in such a way that consciences are sharpened. Even for unbelievers, the fear of the Lord leads to wisdom and integrity, producing godly convictions from a righteous moral compass.

GOOD WORKS

Another important application of this prayer is found in the Sermon on the Mount, the context of the Lord's Prayer.

> *"You are the light of the world. A city set on a hill cannot be hidden. Nor do people light a lamp and put it under a basket, but on a stand, and it gives light to all in the house. In the same way, let your light shine before others, so that they may see your good works and give glory to your Father who is in heaven."* Mt 5:14-16

Glory comes to our Father in Heaven when the Church is active and consistent in good works. This is a part of how we are called to serve the world around us: to be salt and light, which is an influence for truth and morality, but also abounding in good works that flow out of mercy. This goes hand in hand with the signs and wonders that the Church does when it is filled with the power of the Spirit. While the early Church was an excellent example of a supernatural lifestyle, they also excelled in good works as they quickly established feeding programs for the widows among them. This has always been a part of what we are called to do: demonstrate God's love by acts of mercy and service.

These various expressions of mercy and good works need prayer, so that they can be effective and fruitful, but also so that they remain an expression of the gospel. The temptation is to become simply a social service, separated from the message of Jesus. But the Church's good works are meant to be a tangible, ongoing illustration of the love of God, pointing people to the Father, and giving him great glory.

ALL THE NAMES OF GOD

Let's turn for a moment to consider the last word in the petition, "Hallowed be your name". I have already mentioned that a person's name (in a biblical world view), often reflects their prominent characteristic. This may be why there are many names for God found in scripture. Each one of these names is worthy of being hallowed in our lives, families and churches. We've spent time exploring the name "Father," because this is the opening of the prayer and the relational revelation from which the whole prayer flows. But all the other names of God are also worthy of being honoured because they also reveal more of who our God is, his character and nature. (If the Lord is drawing you to pray this way, don't get bogged down with worry about which is a name of the Father, Son or Spirit—they are all one and all God.)

For example, at times you may pray that the Lord, who reveals himself as the Good Shepherd, would shepherd you. This would mean that you would be well shepherded through places where you are unsure of the path and as you go, the needs of rest, peace, restoration and spiritual food would all be met. Then even beyond this, it's a request that those around us would marvel at his goodness and skill as a shepherd when they look at our lives. This would bring glory to the name of the Good Shepherd. Consider the other biblical names of God and what they reveal. The Holy Spirit may highlight a name of God that would express how he particularly wants to minister to you.

APPLYING IT IN PRAYER

As we did with the opening words, "Our Father", here are a few different ways you could pray this first petition, "Hallowed be your name". This is meant to be a way to open the prayer up, not to give you a list of all the ways it *needs* to be prayed, but some suggestions of possibilities. The Holy Spirit will lead and inspire you if you ask him.

- Father, may I be more like Jesus—passionate for you to receive glory
- May my motivations, words and deeds all add to your glory and honour
- Empower me to make your name holy in my life
- Search my heart, show me if there is anything in my life that dishonours you
- Show me any ways I have been taking your glory for myself
- I lay down my "right" to be honoured, noticed or praised
- Show me if I have been giving your glory to another (a leader, a ministry, etc.)
- Pour out in my life, my church and my community more of the Spirit of the fear of the Lord
- May the fear of the Lord lead us into greater integrity and holiness
- May the fear of the Lord soften the hearts of unbelievers in my region, preparing them to hear the gospel
- May my church be filled with testimonies of your supernatural power and miracles
- Let our lives demonstrate that there is power in the name of Jesus
- Let worship be glorious, deep and authentic
- Crown your people with the spirit of praise; may it mark us in good times and bad
- Grant us your compassion for the poor and oppressed, that we may be effective in doing good works to serve them

- Bless and multiply the impact and scope of good works initiated by the Church; may they reflect Jesus to our region and beyond
- May your name be hallowed by many souls being saved

SCRIPTURES TO MEDITATE ON

- How majestic is your name—Ps 8
- Be exalted—Ps 57:11
- Vindicate the holiness of my name—Ezek 36:23
- Call upon the name—Zeph 3:9
- The earth will be filled—Hab 2:14
- The fear of the Lord—Ps 111:10
- The Sprit of the fear of the Lord—Isa 11:2,3
- Glorify the Father—Mt 5:16
- Glorify your name—Rev 15:3,4
- Walk worthy—Col 1:10
- Name above every name—Phil 2:9
- Sanctify the Church—Eph 5:26
- Transformed—2 Cor 3:18

GROUP DISCUSSION QUESTIONS:

1. When you pray, "may your name be hallowed in my life and through my life", are there some areas that the Holy Spirit immediately brings to mind that He wants to help you with?
2. What does the fear of the Lord look like in your life?
3. How could your church's "good works that glorify the Father" be more impactful in your community? Do you have a role in this?

Chapter Five

YOUR KINGDOM COME

We've now arrived at the most popular part of the prayer. This is the petition that gets prayed, preached and sung in so many ways, for it resonates at the deepest level of our hearts as a cry for more of him and all he brings. We intrinsically know we were made to participate in the greatness of his kingdom that we now pray for. There is an echo of Eden that continues to ring in our hearts and this petition puts it into words. As a testimony to the divine source of this prayer, here in three words, the Lord is able to provide a voice for the Church's ache for full unbroken union with him, then using the same words, mobilize the unrelenting thrust into missions and at the same time, awaken a fiery hope for justice, redemption and glory. Three simple, intensely potent words: "Your kingdom come."

The prayer of "Your kingdom come" is intercession, contending for the expansion and advancement of the kingdom of God into all the world with the transforming power of the gospel becoming more prevalent in every nation, demographic and sphere of society.

This kingdom advance is always through the door of the heart. While the kingdoms of this world are all administered through external influences and pressures, Jesus rules and advances his kingdom through hearts being continually encountered and transformed by him. In the kingdom of God, every advance begins with the heart.

> *"Keep your heart with all diligence, for out of it spring the issues of life." Prov 4:23 (NKJV).*

> *"For with the heart one believes and is justified..." Rom 10:10*

> *"...the kingdom of God is within you." Lk 17:21 (NKJV)*

It's absolutely important to grasp that while the kingdom comes to the heart, the vehicle it comes through is the gospel. So, if we have a distorted or reduced understanding of the gospel, there will be no authentic zeal for its increase in our prayers. Instead, we will be relying upon other means to advance the kingdom, be it marketing, self-help/sin-management or obtaining influence through wielding political power and wealth. But the gospel alone brings the kingdom. The gospel is much more than what we've reduced it to; it's the total good news of Jesus Christ, his work, his person, his teaching and his activity right now. He is the King of this kingdom; you cannot have this kingdom without his gospel.

If we, for whatever reason, try to gain the fruit of the kingdom without the gospel being at the core and being the change agent, our efforts end up externally focused, man-exalting and eventually futile. Without heart change there is no authentic transformation and regardless of how much we strive, hearts can't be truly changed by anything other than Jesus and the power of his cross. If there was another way, Jesus wouldn't have had to die. This is why Paul declared to the Corinthians that "he decided to know nothing among them except Jesus Christ and him crucified."[40]

With these big ideas in mind: the kingdom comes through hearts

---

40 1 Cor 2:2

that yield and the gospel is the vehicle the kingdom rides in on, let's now apply them to the Prayer. Let's consider how we can pray "Your kingdom come" in a way that more truly aligns with this understanding and launches into this petition with zealous faith, the type of faith that is absolutely fitting for the glory of this request.

GREAT COMMISSION

In the same way that the Lord's Prayer is linked with the Great Commandment (see Chapter Four), it is here also linked with the Great Commission. This petition pours intercession into the call to "go," the call that has activated outreach, evangelism and foreign missions since the beginning of the Church.

"Go therefore and make disciples of all nations, baptizing them in the name of the Father, and the Son and the Holy Spirit, teaching them to observe all that I've commanded you."[41] It's a prayer for missions, but also for discipleship (including baptism and instruction in all the ways of Jesus) to be successful, speedy, and multiplying everywhere.

Imagine for a moment the explosive way the gospel could fill the nations if the Church fervently laid hold of the call to prayer contained in these three words. If we applied ourselves to pray wholeheartedly for the missions movement, the result would be unprecedented fruit and impact. Souls would be saved, everywhere. The power of the gospel would be fully released in the measure that we see in Mark's account of the Great Commission: *"And he said to them, 'Go into all the world and proclaim the gospel to the whole creation. Whoever believes and is baptized will be saved, but whoever does not believe will be condemned. And these signs will accompany those who believe: in my name they will cast out demons; they will speak in new tongues; they will pick up serpents with their hands; and if they drink any deadly poison, it will not hurt them; they will lay their hands on the sick, and they will recover.'"*[42]

---

41 Mt 28:19-20
42 Mk 15:16-18

An awakening of prayer would open extraordinary doors for effective ministry to all evangelistic endeavors. Hearts would be softened and prepared to hear the Good News. There would be supernatural favour on the proclamation of the gospel, which would open up new access to demographics once closed and resistant to the name of Jesus. Unreached people groups would finally hear of God's love for them. This would be our story if the whole Church would only pray "Your kingdom come," with faith.

This prayer is also intercession for the power of the Holy Spirit to fill all the discipleship endeavours that are an integral part of the Great Commission. It pushes past the non-biblical concept of making converts and church attendees, who rarely look little different than their secular neighbours. It reaches for the kingdom mandate to replicate the life of Christ in all who choose to follow him. It's the transforming gospel applied to hearts, again and again and again, by the power of the Spirit. How desperately we need intercession for this aspect of the Great Commission. It is the challenge of the Church to lead all believers, both brand new and those who have followed him for years, into becoming wholly kingdom people.

For the kingdom to advance it will go broader into new places and encountering new people, but it will also go deeper, with the gospel maturing, sanctifying, strengthening and activating the Body of Christ. But there is more. The kingdom is supernatural and powerful. When the kingdom comes, it brings healing, deliverance and jaw-dropping miracles into lives. This is also a prayer for the supernatural reality of the kingdom to come from heaven to earth; all that the kingdom is, springing up and flourishing in our midst.

If we think about the expansiveness of the kingdom of God, its features or attributes, we begin to have a very extensive list. Wherever these attributes are lacking, praying for the kingdom to come can specifically focus prayer on this need.

Let's think about the attributes of the kingdom of God. What does it look like when God is moving among us? What changes? What does the kingdom bring? Here is a list to get you started envisioning more of the kingdom. Essentially, the kingdom of God looks like Jesus in charge and who he is breaking forth everywhere as his good, wise leadership causes true shalom in our lives and communities. As you look over this list, think of how each of these attributes in full expression could look. Allow your vision of the kingdom of God to expand and the burden of prayer for its coming to grow in your heart.

Attributes of the Kingdom of God:

- **Redemption**—Jesus is our Redeemer, so his kingdom is full of redemption. There is always hope when he's involved; He never leaves us in dead-end situations. He'll even give us beauty for our ashes (Isa 61:3).
- **Wisdom**—The kingdom of God is full of wisdom that is pure, peaceable, gentle, open to reason, full of mercy and good fruits, impartial, and sincere (Jas 3:17). It flows out of the root of the fear of the Lord (Prov. 9:10).
- **Peace**—Jesus' just, wise, government brings unending peace wherever it's established (Isa 9:7). Peace is even a dominant sign of his kingdom, along with righteousness, and joy—in the Holy Spirit (Rom 14:17).
- **Grace**—Jesus is full of grace and truth (Jn 1:14). His kingdom is the New Covenant which is not established by us perfectly fulfilling the law, but by trusting in his grace. Everything in Jesus' kingdom is marked by this beautiful grace (Rom 6:14).
- **Beauty**—You only have to look at creation to see the exquisite beauty that has its source in God. Even marred by sin, it's an ongoing testimony of who he is; a beautiful God. He continues to create and build his kingdom with stunning beauty (Ps 19:1, Ps 27:4).

- **Truth**—Jesus is the Truth and reveals absolute truthful reality to us (Jn 14:6). He lifts us out of the ravages of lies, deception and distortion; he sets our feet on the bedrock of all truth, the revelation of the nature of God.
- **Holiness**—Holiness is integrally woven into the fabric of the kingdom of God, for God is holy. He is continually sanctifying his people, setting them free from sin and giving them the righteousness of the Lamb of God (I Pt 2:9).
- **Justice**—God is perfectly just and so his kingdom will also be perfectly just when fully established (Rev 16:5). As we are currently in the "now and not yet" time, where the kingdom is here, yet not fully here, we see justice shining forth most brightly where his kingdom is the strongest (Isa 33:5).
- **Provision**—Because God reveals himself as our provider, there will always be full provision in his kingdom. At times it might be extravagant abundance, while at other times more modest, yet it's always what we need (Gen 22:14, Mt 6:25-33).
- **Mercy**—Not only do we receive mercy, fresh and renewed every day but the kingdom of God includes the people of God ministering the Father's mercy into the world (Lam 3:22-23, Mt 9:12-13).
- **Healing**—Jesus healed wherever He went and continues to heal today. Whether bodies, souls, hearts, relationships or minds… his kingdom is marked with healing (Lk 6:19, 4:18).
- **Unity**—The Trinity exist in complete oneness and Jesus is building his Church into the same quality of unity. Expect the kingdom of God to draw us out of isolation, independence and division (Jn 17:21-23).
- **Miracles**—The kingdom is coming from heaven to earth, so as it does, the supernatural interrupts normal life. Jesus

walked in miraculous ways and declared his disciples would do greater things (Jn 14:12).

- **Generosity**—The Father gave the Son, the Son gave his life. Nothing about God is stingy. Sacrificial generosity is a sign of the kingdom, it's a sign that God's nature is flowing through his people (Rom 8:32).
- **Love**—Perhaps the most obvious attribute of God's kingdom is love. God is love and all who follow him seek to obey two primary commandments: love God and love your neighbour as yourself (Mk 12:29-31).
- **Dignity**—While the kingdom is not about us demanding dignity in a prideful way, the Father clothes us in dignity where we once lived in shame. We are clothed in the favour of the Son; where the kingdom goes, people created in the image of God are restored to dignity (Lk 15:22).
- **Abundant life**—The kingdom of God involves abiding in Christ, the source of indestructible life (Heb 7:16). Because he is our source, our lives and indeed the entire community of the people of God, will exhibit the richness and fullness of our life-giving God (Jn 10:10).
- **Joy**—The kingdom of God is righteousness, peace and joy in the Holy Spirit. Expect much joy, even in the midst of hardship and struggle (Rom 14:17, Jas 1:2).
- **Creativity**—The first revelation of God is as Creator, so we can expect his kingdom to continue to be marked by creativity. He continually inspires his redeemed people with rich expressions of original creativity as we reflect the image of our Creator (Col 1:16).
- **Hope**—As leaders in the early Church wrote the scriptures, they consistently spoke of hope, especially the hope of the resurrection. The reality of our certain future profoundly colours

our present reality and should wash us of all hopelessness or despair (1 Pt 1:3-5). God's kingdom is marked by indomitable hope.

- **Authority**—Jesus is seated on the throne of heaven far above all earthly power or rule. His authority flows into his kingdom, but not in a domineering way; he always graciously honours our free will (Phil 2:9,10).
- **Power**—"The kingdom of God is not [just] words, but power" (1 Cor 4:20). It involves power over every demonic stronghold of darkness, every grip sin has had in our lives and even death itself. Jesus also clothes his people with the power of the Spirit to fulfill his commission (Acts 1:8).
- **Fruitfulness**—In the beginning we were called to be fruitful and multiply (Gen 1:28). As we abide in the Vine (Jesus), we gain the ability to fulfill that original mandate. Jesus' kingdom is always growing and advancing (Mt 11:12). Even though there are seasons of pruning, fruitfulness is the norm in the kingdom of God.
- **Light**—There is no darkness in God and likewise, his people are called to walk in the light, bringing his light to the world around us. Holiness, transparency, the light of revelation and glory are all aspects of his light (1 Jn 1:5-7).
- **Purpose**—The kingdom of God flows out of the will of the Father, which is to bring about the restoration of all things in his Son. Nothing in the kingdom is pointless, random, futile or in vain. Where the kingdom of God abounds, vision, restored purpose and life callings all become clear (Eph 2:10).

Where there is a lack of any of these attributes of the kingdom, praying, "Your kingdom come," becomes a prayer that is applied to that specific lack. The more we ask for the kingdom to come, the more these signs of God's presence and the working of his hand will become noticeable around us, for this is a prayer he will always answer.

IT'S HIS KINGDOM, NOT OURS

The kingdom we are asking for is a kingdom that belongs to Jesus. He has been enthroned over heaven and earth; there is no peer who can challenge his throne. He will reign with absolute sovereignty and authority forever. Yet with all of this power, he still graciously invites us to yield to his leadership, which is his kingship. When we pray, "Your kingdom come", this can be a moment of deep surrender and full allegiance with his kingship in our lives.

We often act like little kings wanting control over our lives, our obedience to Jesus depending on his will lining up with ours. We may allow him to be Lord over a few areas of our lives, but hold back others, reserving our right to have the final say. Daily praying "Your kingdom come," yields the direction of our lives to the Father and invites his kingship in fuller and greater ways in every area of our lives.

In the book of Joshua there are many accounts of military conflicts between Israel and their enemies. This can be a picture of the struggle to submit areas of our lives to Christ. As we do submit, like the lands Israel conquered, they become territory where God is King. It's a beautiful prayer to ask the Lord for his kingdom to rule in areas of our lives that have been stubbornly unyielding. Although we will likely have to pray this repeatedly to thoroughly establish a submitted heart (for we slip back into self-rule in our moments of weakness), it is worth the fight for Jesus to have more "territory" in our lives. His reign will bring peace, health and life. Praying, "Your kingdom come," into finances, relationships or eating habits (as examples), are wonderful ways to apply this prayer.

At times the desire for control over our own lives extends to wanting to control others and our environment. This could involve the direction our church is going, the career choices that our children are making or many other issues. Remembering that it's his kingdom not ours means we relinquish to him any tendencies to try to manipulate or control others. We let him lead his kingdom as he sees fit, not according to our preferences. If this one petition was embraced and this one posture of surrender to his kingship was practiced, we would find the ungodly control that has so wounded lives and marred the Church lifted. This in itself would result in the life of God bursting forth, as we stopped trying to control both others and outcomes, either subtly or overtly.

SERVANT OF ALL KINGDOM

Jesus didn't use his powerful personality in a fleshly way to manipulate others into following him; he trusted the Father. In fact, he introduced a radical new way to lead others with the stunning concept of "*he who wants to be great in the kingdom must be the servant of all.*"[43]

As we wrestle with our hearts to give him full and continuous Lordship, we also wrestle to lay down our desire to wield fleshly power.

This concept of servant leadership was unheard of when Christ introduced it and even to the disciples who walked most closely with him, initially, it made no sense. The idea that the way up is down, the way to increase is to be poured out and the way to truly live is to die to self, were all spiritual principles that they, like us, struggled with. They were accustomed to leaders who asserted and promoted themselves, who jockeyed for position and prominence, catered to the rich and powerful and trampled on those they had no use for; leaders who looked to the matrix of fame, money and political influence as the road to power. Even after Jesus' resurrection, the disciples were still expecting him to grasp political power and establish an earthly kingdom in Israel.

When we pray for God's kingdom to come, we too can be confused about what his dominion on earth looks like. It's easy to use a worldly paradigm, where the path to the kingdom would be achieved by positioning Christians in the most influential seats of power, so they can

---

43 Mk 10:43

bring God's righteousness and values to our world. This would be a simple top-down approach where we could expect a trickling down of positive change. But this view forgets that without Christ transforming our hearts, our deeds are evil and we continue to love darkness. Even if there are righteous people in influential positions, without revival creating widespread heart change, the righteousness of leaders will be resisted and rebelled against rather than embraced.

While God at times uses men and women positioned strategically for extraordinary purposes like modern day Esthers or Josephs, the kingdom of God flows through hearts. It's from revived and transformed hearts that it overflows into the rest of our lives and then our world. The kingdom of God is an upside-down kingdom in the sense that it's about serving rather than lusting for power; it's an inside-out kingdom, coming from his law written on softened hearts, as opposed to people being pressured to conform to Christian-oriented laws, values and morals.

Jesus the King is remarkable in the way he chose to walk in humility, making himself accessible to the most broken and despised in our society. He invites us to follow in this path and to pray for the Church to daily choose this narrow way, rather than the broad way of the world.

A JUST KINGDOM

The kingdom that Jesus brings and the kingdom we are praying for is one of justice. It is a kingdom where all that has been shattered or defiled by sin will ultimately be restored when he returns. But as we wait for this to be accomplished, we are called to be actively participating in his mission of justice. This is justice for the oppressed: those who are living under the grinding heel of systemic poverty, those who are enslaved, those who are suffering under injustice or tragedy.

Jesus began his ministry by stepping into the call of Isaiah 61:1-2, declaring he was anointed to bring liberty to captives and good news to the poor.[44] He then went on to embrace those who had been shunned by society, making radical social statements of his inclusion of all people. Paul and the other Apostles caught his heart and emphasized their shared value of remembering the poor. [45] Even Jesus' brother, James, teaches us that the evidence of the kingdom of God (true religion) is good works, especially those done on behalf of widows and orphans.[46]

Scripture, in the Old and New Testament alike, paints an unmistakable picture of God's kingdom being a one of justice where the poor, the refugee and the oppressed are cared for.

We can certainly add to this the cause of caring for the environment, God's creation, with stewardship and wisdom. But while the Church is called to serve in these areas and be a corrective, prophetic voice in the halls of power, we must walk in humility and love, avoiding self-righteousness. We are pursuing the redemption of *all*, the oppressed and the oppressor. Our work in social justice is full of God's compassion and justice, but it can never be separated from the truth of the person, work and message of Jesus.

THE RETURN OF THE KING

Even with all our good works, full justice will only come when the King returns. Praying "Your kingdom come" aligns us with the final cry of Revelation 22:17, "The Spirit and the Bride say, 'Come'." This is the great yearning of the Church: the return of her glorious Bridegroom-King. Praying "Your kingdom come" becomes a part of the global river of prayer, flowing since the birth of the Church; God's people crying in one voice, "Maranatha: come quickly Jesus."

We who live in the Western world, enjoying a more comfortable and convenient Christianity, may find this prayer for the return of Christ a bit challenging. It flies in the face of temporal values as in

44 Lk 4:18
45 Gal 2:10
46 Jas 1:27

the parable of the rich land owner found in Luke 12:16-21. In this passage Jesus teaches about a man whose life's ambition was to gain wealth and security for the sole objective of his personal pleasure. In the parable he says to his soul, "Soul, you have ample goods laid up for many years: relax, eat, drink, be merry." But God calls him a fool because he's squandered his life pursuing something that has infinitely less value than the kingdom of God.

If we don't long for Christ's return or we secretly hope that it's delayed, we find in this prayer a call to realign with eternal values. Praying it gives us time to take stock of what really matters and disconnect from the frantic pursuit of materialism that dominates our society.

APPLYING IT IN PRAYER

At this point I want to suggest some ways to apply this petition personally or in an intercessory way for others. Let these prayer points be a resource to draw from as the Holy Spirit leads you to pray for God's kingdom to come on earth, as it is in heaven.

- May I receive your leadership in greater measure to my life, family and church
- I yield to your kingship in all things
- Open our spiritual eyes to the revelation of the splendour of your kingship; may we worship in awe as the angels do
- Let the gospel go forth in effective, anointed ways in my region, so that those who have never heard will now hear
- Show me ways I can expand your kingdom in my community
- Back up the true preaching of the gospel with extraordinary signs and wonders
- Stretch out your hand to heal and do miracles through your Church; may we be known as a supernatural people
- Release the attributes of your kingdom within your Church,

that we would be empowered and resourced by you

- May the justice of your kingdom break into the situations of oppression around me
- May the creativity of your kingdom burst forth, bringing heavenly solutions and beauty
- Influence our government toward laws and priorities that are righteous and reflect your heart
- May your people, whom you have strategically placed to be salt and light in our society, have favour
- May the lives of your people reflect your kingdom life, that we may give light, like a city on a hill
- Increase my trust in your kingship and sovereignty, even when it feels like everything is out of control
- Awaken a fresh, authentic longing for your return—come, Lord Jesus
- Help us to lay down our desire for personal power and position and follow you into servanthood
- Empower us to make disciples who will be conduits of healing, redemption, freedom and transformation
- Grant us your vision and passion for the fulfillment of the Great Commission

SCRIPTURES TO MEDITATE ON

- At hand—Mt 10:7,8
- Repent—Mt 3:2
- Healing and proclamation—Mt 4:23
- Good soil—Mk 4:20
- Like a child—Lk 18:17

- Righteousness, peace and joy—Rom 14:17
- Seek first—Mt 6:33
- Father's good pleasure—Lk 12:32
- Produce the fruit of the kingdom—Mt 21:43
- Not talk but power—1 Cor 4:20
- Not of this world—Jn 18:36
- Walk worthy—1 Thes 2:12
- Servant of all—Lk 22:26
- Beatitudes—Mt 5:3-10
- Endure forever—Dan 2:44, 6:26
- Unshakable—Heb 12:28
- Advancing—Mt 11:12
- Throne of God—Rev 4:2-11
- Our kingdom commission—Mt 28:19,20
- A kingdom of priests—Rev 5:10
- Come Lord Jesus—Rev 22:20
- To every nation—Mt 24:14
- King of kings—Rev 19:16

GROUP DISCUSSION QUESTIONS:

1. What are some supernatural manifestations of the kingdom that you are now inspired to pray for?
2. How does thinking about Jesus as your King make you feel?
3. Do you live in an anticipation of Jesus' second coming? Why or why not?

Chapter Six

YOUR WILL BE DONE

The last petition in the opening trinity of God-ward requests is a cry for God's will to be done.

These four words, "Your will be done" like the preceding "Your kingdom come," are packed with revelation, bringing greater clarity and understanding to foundational truths about prayer. One key foundational truth, which becomes so essential when learning to pray, is that God's will can be known. It was Jesus who gave us the Lord's Prayer, so his life is the context by which we understand its meaning. The prayer is not disjointed from what Christ taught, how he lived or what he brought by way of radical change.

Jesus modelled a life where he knew the will of God, embraced it, and perfectly obeyed it. The Book of Hebrews, quoting Jesus says, "I have come to do your will O God."[47] In John's gospel, Jesus again tells his disciples that he only does what he sees the Father doing and only speaks what he hears the Father saying.[48] These confident assertions would have been impossible to make if the will of God had been obscured in any way.

---

47 Heb 10:7

48 Jn 5:19, 12:49

Like Jesus, we too can know the will of God and fervently pray with bold faith. This is how Jesus prayed and what he's expecting us to pursue as we pray this petition. Sadly, praying "Your will be done" has often been approached as either praying in a fatalistic way of "whatever happens, happens" or in a big, ambiguous, benevolent wish over the earth, which requires no heart engagement or faith.

Both of these approaches fall short of how Jesus prayed and how he instructed us to pray, even though they are common and widespread. Let's look at them in more detail and then explore how to go beyond them to find breakthrough.

The Fatalist Approach: "Whatever happens, happens"

This is an approach that disconnects us from faith and active intercession, positioning us in a passive posture. While on the surface it may sound like yielding to God's will, it's actually an indifference to the outcome and a presumption that all that occurs is ultimately God's desire. This is so different from the walk of intimacy and understanding of God's will that Jesus modelled. A subtle way that we can slip into this prayer pitfall is when we ask the Father for something and then walk back our request as our faith starts to waver, by adding "if it be your will". The end result is double-minded prayer.

Far better to pursue him for the revelation of his will and in as much as that revelation is granted, then pray with full faith for what he shows is his desire. For sure, there are times when we just don't know and so we pray more carefully to avoid stepping into presumption, but this is much different from an apathetic passiveness to his will being done.

Jesus was zealously committed to the Father's will. He sought it out and his life on earth was the perfect embodiment of, "I delight to do your will O Lord."[49]

---

49 Ps 40:8

The Benevolent Wish Approach

With this approach we have no need for faith because we are just using "Your will be done" as a general, ambiguous blessing over everything. This is like praying, "may God's love bless the world." If God's will is to be manifest on the earth, it needs to have a touchdown point; it needs to encounter the earth in real time and space, just as Jesus stepped into actual time and space through the incarnation. Without a tangible application, there is no place for faith to be activated or stretched. There is no need for faith to secure a victory.

The kingdom grows through believing in Jesus more and more, with every advance of the kingdom coming by grace though faith. Hebrews tells us that without faith it's impossible to please God.[50] So how do we apply faith to this petition of "Your will be done"? It requires as much as possible, discerning the revealed will of God and activating our faith to believe that if we ask the Father for a request that is in accordance with his will, he both hears us and grants our requests.[51]

REVEALED IN SCRIPTURE

The macro themes of God's plans and intentions are revealed throughout scripture, from Genesis to Revelation. They surface again and again, woven though the stories, laws, letters and prophecies. They illustrate that God is undeterred and unrelenting in accomplishing his will, regardless of the setbacks or delays because of the disobedience of his people. These same revealed plans and purposes echo though our lives as well and as we learn from scripture, we gain a greater understanding of what we are moving toward. For example, it's his will to dwell among us. He revealed this in the beginning in the Garden; he's never deviated from this intention and it will be magnificently accomplished in fullness through his Son. We move closer to this every day.

---

50 Heb 11:6
51 1 Jn 5:14

There are many of these macro themes that we can consider and they can be expressed in a variety of ways. As you pray the Lord's Prayer, it's likely that the Spirit will highlight one or more of these themes of his will for you to zero in on. I've listed some themes below to get you started, bearing in mind there are many more that could be considered.

THE WILL OF GOD

- For God to tangibly and gloriously dwell with man—Ex 25:8, Eph 2:22, Rev 21:3
- That none would perish—1 Tim 2:4, Lk 19:10, Jn 3:17
- For the Church to represent God to the world—2 Cor 5:18-20, Mt 5:14-16, Col 1:25-28
- For there to be perfect unity in the Church—Jn 17:11, 21-23, Eph 4:3-6
- For marriages and families to be strong and healthy—Eph 5:31,32, Gen 2:24, Heb 13:4
- For the gospel to be proclaimed to every nation, in every language—Mt 24:14, Mt 28:19,20, Rev 7:9,10
- That we would love God and love one another—Mt 22:37-39
- For the Church to become a glorious, mature bride, without spot or wrinkle—Eph 5:27, Rev 19:7, 1Pt 2:9-12
- For the Lord's house to become a house of prayer, open to all—Isa 56:7, Mk 11:17, Acts 2:41,42
- For justice to be established on earth—Isa 42:1, Lk 11:7, Isa 9:7
- That we would be conformed to the image of the Son—1 Jn 3:2,3, Rom 8:29, 2 Cor 3:18
- For the name of Jesus to be exalted above every other name—Dan 7:14, Phil 2:9,10, Eph 1:20-22

As you pray through these macro themes, look for the places of application—places where the kingdom and will of God need to break in all around you. Admittedly, it's much less painful to be detached and disengaged from the real life, in-the-trenches needs that demand faith, compassion and perseverance to carry in prayer. But this is not how Jesus walked, nor is it how his kingdom advances. We must allow the burden of the brokenness and needs around us to touch our hearts, so that we can be moved by compassion. At times, tears are the most powerful form of prayer. If we are willing to engage with his burdens, he grants a deeper understanding of his will, his timing and his ways, empowering us to effectively partner with him in intercession.

It's in these rubber-hits-the-road situations where you can see the answers to prayer so clearly. Without praying for real people with real needs, your faith is not authentically applied or challenged to grow. This leaves you robbed of the God-stories, (the testimonies of answered prayer) and the celebration and great encouragement they bring. These answers to prayer are very important, as recounting them uniquely builds faith, courage and endurance in all who hear.

For example, in the last months, I've been praying for a miracle. We live in BC's Lower Mainland, the most expensive area in the nation for housing; a place where, even with a good job (unless you bought a house years ago), suitable housing for a family is largely out of reach. Our son, along with his wife and four young children, needed to move out of their current rental home. My husband and I would look at the listings, for rental or purchase, and shake our heads—the prices were sky-high, and continuing to rise. Bidding wars for properties coming on the market were driving these high prices even higher and pressuring buyers or renters to pounce on anything listed that could possibly accommodate them.

Our family prayed, our church prayed and I prayed daily, looking to the Lord—whose name is still Provider regardless of what the housing market is doing. "Father, you provide daily bread, you provided manna out of nothing—provide for our son and his family; their trust is in you." In spite of the prices, we had to believe the Father was able. Of course, you can guess the end of this story! In a few weeks they'll move into their new home in the exact neighbourhood they wanted, with the yard, the four bedrooms and even the brand new kitchen they had dreamed of.

It took standing in faith, but now this testimony builds faith in everyone who hears.

DISCERNED BY THE SPIRIT

Let's go back for a moment to the concept that the Spirit grants deeper revelation to the specifics of the Father's will as we pray. This is something we addressed at length in Chapter Two, so suffice it to say that we must constantly train ourselves to lean into the Spirit, rather than leaning on our own analysis of the situation. We want to pray according to the Father's will and the Spirit will surely help us if we pay attention to him and are responsive to his nudges.

The Father will speak to us about his will for our lives and to a degree, may give us discernment of his will for the lives and situations of others. An important principle is to hold our own discernment, especially for others, loosely, rather than trying to enforce it, while at the same time recognizing the greater the burden for these situations is, the more we are being called to invest prayer.

You can see that discerning the Father's will is more of an art than a science. It's an art that requires growing in spiritual maturity and intimacy with the Lord, as we learn how to listen to the Holy Spirit who is seeking to help us in our weakness. It's a journey where we all misunderstand what we've heard at times, so we can't be afraid of getting it wrong here and there; that's part of learning. As we keep walking, Jesus helps us to grow in hearing his voice. It's a journey that we are all invited into, not just those who are particularly gifted in discernment or prophecy. When Jesus said, "My sheep hear my voice" he was referring to *all* of his sheep.[52] If hearing his voice and knowing his will for you has been a struggle, seek to spend more time in the scriptures, ask him to help you hear and listen to the Holy Spirit with expectant faith.

PERSEVERING PRAYER

Once the will of God has been clearly discerned and confirmed, prayer that is both faith-filled and unwavering should rise in our hearts. It's not enough to know the will of God and enjoy being brought into his confidences; this revelation is given to equip us for action. This is the time to be fully, passionately, invested in seeing the will of God done, not ambivalent or lukewarm.

Consider the image of persevering prayer that Jesus gave us in the now-familiar parable of the friend at midnight. What we see illustrated is a relentless, audacious asking, knocking, seeking, until the answer is yes. The slight brush off, "it's too much bother," (my paraphrase) is essentially ignored by the knocking neighbour. In his mind, no is not an option; he will continue knocking until the neighbour yields and grants his request.

The early Church practiced this type of urgent, intense intercession as well. A great example is when they gathered to pray for Peter's release from prison in Acts 12:5. Consider the setting: the fledgling church had just lost one of their primary leaders, James, the brother of John, to martyrdom. This would have been incredibly traumatic. James was known to them all and deeply loved. He was one of the three who was most intimately discipled by Jesus and walked in great revelation of the ways of Christ, which he would have been imparting to the young, hungry Church. His death had come on the heels of the painful loss of Stephen, the revivalist deacon, who was brutally stoned to death. Now Peter, the de facto leader of the Church, had been seized and was on "death row", with everyone expecting that in a matter of days, he too would be martyred.

---

52 Jn 10:27

The Church knew it was not the will of God for Peter to die at this time and they gathered to earnestly pray. When we drill down to look at this word, "earnestly" in the original Greek (ektenēs), we find it implies that they were praying both fervently and without ceasing—late into the night. This was a life or death prayer meeting and they were determined to knock until the door opened. Then as we see in the following verses, open it did.

When we know the will of God and are facing a situation that is contrary, we have the same call to pray with fervency and persistence until we see things change. But a word of caution here: it is vital to hold our revelation of the discerned will of God in a posture of humility. "We know in part and we prophecy in part";[53] meaning that we draw from spiritual revelation to fill in that which we don't know, but there is always the aspect of mixture in our spiritual revelation. We discern and interpret what we discern through the lens of our humanity which can cloud our revelation. With this in mind, when you discern the will of God, pursue it vigorously in prayer, yet keep listening to the Lord to clarify or even redirect your intercession. You cannot shut your ears and insist your will upon the Father. He will not be moved by your fasting, intensity of intercession, decrees or prophetic actions if you are insisting on something that is not his will.

We must always remember that he is God and we are not. He understands the beginning from the end and delights to use us in prayer, by revealing his will to us. But if this becomes inverted and we demand that he serve our will—we can expect to be disappointed. We also must remember that while he generously gives us revelation to lead us into effective prayer, this is a glimpse rather than us fully seeing, knowing and understanding. Humility in handling revelation is most fitting.

With all this said, there are still occasions when the Father withholds revelation for a time, or even completely. In these times we are being trained in trust. We just don't know, despite all our asking and seeking for revelation. Yet in this place we can still pray for his will to

---

53 1 Cor 13:9

be done, with full faith and hearts confident that he's responding to our prayer. We're just doing it sight unseen.

"The secrets of the Lord are with those that fear him."[54] In this passage, the psalmist links revelation with the fear (reverence) of the Lord. This is a key scripture, demonstrating the importance of the fear of the Lord as we handle revelation. Revelation draws us into passionate, bold prayer, but it's the fear of the Lord that keeps us from overstepping in presumption, pressing him for what is actually our will or a misconstruing of his.

SURRENDER

I mentioned earlier in this chapter that Jesus knew and delighted in doing the will of the Father, but he also modelled surrendering to the Father's will even when it was costly. Praying "Your will be done" should remind us of Jesus' own prayer in Gethsemane, "Father, if you are willing, remove this cup from me. Nevertheless, not my will but yours be done."[55] Here we see the most supreme example of yielding human will to the will of God. This prayer was utter surrender to, and trust in the Father, an example that leaves us in awe when we consider the cup that he was being handed.

No one has suffered as deeply as Jesus did in his crucifixion. Even with the horror he saw when looking into the cup the Father was giving him, he postured his heart not just in submission, but trust. Jesus trusted the Father to work out the greatness and goodness of his plan even while facing excruciating darkness and agony. It was for the joy set before him that he endured the cross and he was confident that joy would indeed follow the cross because of his unshakable trust in the Father.

We can't authentically pray "Your will be done" in a different spirit than the profound surrender that Jesus modelled. Even in our weakness,

54 Ps 25:14
55 Lk 22:42

we seek to follow what he has set in motion. Even with conflicted hearts that are not fully given over to his will, we choose this way and seek to grow in Christlike, joyful surrender.

Praying this prayer as a personal prayer of surrender is a practice of daily reconnecting with the will of God. It's nipping in the bud, independence or a worldly pursuing and asserting our own will. It's daily humbling ourselves and renewing intimate dependence on the Father, like branches on the vine. As we pray this prayer it gives the Lord an opportunity to highlight where we have been obeying his will begrudgingly, perhaps resisting it in our hearts or maybe even fully avoiding it.

Often one of the most difficult areas to surrender is to yield to God's timing. We want our blessings quickly; we hate the agonizing "standing in faith" time, where against all hope, (even when there is no indication of God doing anything) we have to believe.[56] Yet he's always accomplishing multiple good purposes at the same time and all his ways are perfect—including his timing.

The early disciples lived in a world very hostile to their faith and consequently, they suffered. This wasn't a surprise to them, as they expected to be treated like their Master. They took Jesus' words that following him meant carrying a cross much more literally than we generally do. The Apostles taught the Church to be courageous in the face of all forms of suffering, persecution and even martyrdom.[57] They saw beyond the momentary light affliction to the glory and fellowship with Christ that their suffering brought.[58] So when we have a path of suffering, let's not be shocked or shaken in our faith. Joyful surrender to God's will, with hearts full of trust, even when it's the cup of suffering that is before us, is an extraordinary love offering to the Father.

The greatest level of surrender to God's will goes even beyond fully submitting to it into allowing the will of God to become *our* burning passion, allowing it to possess *our hearts*. Again, we look to Jesus as our

---

56 Rom 4:18
57 1 Pt 5:10
58 2 Cor 4:17

example. His greatest passions reveal the passion of the Father. He had no independent ambition, but it was said of him, "Zeal for your house consumes me."[59] Likewise, when we read the greatest stories of revival, we encounter those whom the Spirit has drawn into this place of not just a full surrender of their will, but a full possession of their heart, so they are aflame with God's desires and indifferent to their own.

ON EARTH AS IT IS IN HEAVEN

Before we leave this petition of "Your will be done" we want to remember that we are praying for this glorious will of God to be done in the same way that it's done in heaven. In fact, it's not just, "Your will be done," but all three of the opening petitions are connected to this phrase: "On earth as it is in heaven".[60] May the name of the Father be honoured, his kingdom come and his will be done, all in the same way that they are in heaven. This dramatically raises the benchmark of what we are asking for. No longer are we asking for just a slight improvement, but for the full measure of what is in heaven to come to earth.

Let's consider how the will of God is done in heaven, because that is what we are asking for. What's initially obvious is that in heaven, the will of God is always done fully and wholeheartedly. It's also done immediately—there is no angel, living creature or saint who would be distracted with other interests or who would delay obedience to the Father as they wrestle with their own will.

The will of God is also done joyfully and there is a great agreement with the goodness, the justice and the wisdom of God's ways. Praise breaks forth; complaints and murmuring are never heard coming from the lips of the angels. Let's pray that in our lives and in our churches, we will receive and embrace the will of God in the same way as it's received and embraced in heaven! Let's apply ourselves to pray for

59 Jn 2:17

60 Darrell Johnson addresses this concept more throughly in his book, *"Fifty-Seven Words that Change the World: A Journey through the Lord's Prayer"* (Vancouver, British Columbia, Canada: Regent College Publishing, 2005).

heaven's responsiveness to the will of God to be echoed on the earth, becoming the norm in our lives, families and churches.

What a high standard! But rather than making us feel that it's all so unachievable and utopian, let's let this benchmark thrill our spirits as we consider that this prayer will be fully granted. Jesus is building his Church. We are being sanctified, matured and built together into the New Jerusalem, a dwelling place for him with a glorious, coming-from-heaven nature.

When we pray, "On earth as it is in heaven," there are likely a few applications that immediately spring to mind. These may be based on our sense of need or an acute awareness of the brokenness around us. We might think about the fact that there is no sickness or poverty in heaven, so we pray that this will be our earthly reality. But rather than only looking at earth and the needs here, there is great revelation that can come from looking carefully at the most significant features of heaven. This can reorient our prayer and fill us with wonderful hope. These heavenly features are what we ask would manifest here on earth, with the Church like a greenhouse, receiving and nurturing them, but then allowing them to flow out to bless the world around us.

Here are few of the prominent features of heaven, the source and the epicentre of the kingdom of God. If these are not apparent in our setting, we can be alerted that we have drifted from our core calling. We are meant to be embassies of heaven and conduits of the most concentrated and glorious flow of heaven into the earth.

WHAT'S IN HEAVEN?

Heaven hosts the most intense and beautiful holiness of any place. It's a holiness that takes your breath away in awe-filled worship as you fall prostrate before the Lord. This atmosphere and revelation of holiness eternally inspires the four living creatures to unceasingly declare, "Holy,

holy, holy is the Lord God Almighty, who was and is and is to come."[61] In this atmosphere of holiness, there is no flicker of sin, doubt or darkness.

Heaven also hosts the throne of God, the seat of authority over all creation, for all eternity. From here, he rules the universe, the nations, the times and seasons, displaying his majesty, power and glory.

In heaven, every eye is upon Jesus. He is fully revealed and worshiped as the worthy Lamb of God. The wonder and magnitude of his sacrifice and victory are eternally celebrated and honoured. Glory is given to the power of his work on the cross and all of heaven worships him for ransoming his people from every tribe, language and nation. But not only is he redeeming them, he is transforming them into a kingdom of priests wholly devoted to him forever. Heaven celebrates the Lamb receiving the reward of his suffering.

The climate of heaven is one of love; the fullness of God's love revealed without any distortion or filter. Here we finally see the full scope of the height and depth and length and breadth of the love of God. Every person is fully known and profoundly cherished. Joy abounds and is irrepressible.

Heaven is where the Church is revealed as the New Jerusalem. It's perfectly built, every stone in precisely the right place; every aspect stunningly beautiful. It has no shabby or mediocre sections; every part is bursting with splendour, glory and light. Here is the ultimate and the most perfect expression of community and Jesus is at the centre of it all. It is the pinnacle of God dwelling with man.

Perhaps these seem like lofty thoughts and concepts, disconnected from our present reality in this frail and broken life, frustratingly out of reach. Yet this is where we are going! The plan is already in motion. In this prayer we are being invited into God's purposes in a deeper way, for Jesus hasn't called us to just dream of heaven; he's looking for a landing strip, a heart that welcomes the substance of heaven, right here and now. In the beginning we were created out of the dust of the earth, so as

---

61 Rev 4:8

we pray, "On earth as it is in heaven," we are calling all the power and beauty of heaven into our lives, our little patches of earth. As we pray in this way we are opening our hearts and lives to be heaven's colony. Perhaps it begins in small ways, but as we continue to pray and welcome the Lord's kingship, it increases.

He has not given us this prayer to pray as a wistful longing, like exiled old men dreaming of their homeland but helpless to return. Jesus has every intention of bringing the reality and eternity of heaven into our lives, individually and corporately. Whenever you pray the Lord's Prayer in a way that's biblical and full of faith, you can expect him to answer.

APPLYING IT IN PRAYER

With all that we've discussed in this chapter concerning the will of God, let's consider a few of the ways that this simple petition could be applied to our lives.

- Father, show me your will for ______ situation; let me see this from your perspective
- Bring clarity and revelation when I don't know which way to go
- Bring the full revelation of your will to my church
- Show me the wisdom of your will so that I might rejoice in it
- Grant me grace to totally surrender and wholeheartedly follow your will
- Change those situations in my life that are not your will; help me to pray steadfastly until they shift
- Help me to discern your timing and trust you in what feels like a delay
- It is your will that none should perish—draw my neighbour's heart to you

- It is your will that we walk in unity—increase the level of unity in my church
- It is your will that marriages be strong—lead my marriage into greater health and deeper love
- Speak to me through the scriptures and disciple me—I want to wholly follow you
- Show me where I've been unwittingly walking in independence, pursing my own will. Uproot independence from my heart
- I declare your will is good and perfect, even when it involves suffering and much waiting
- Change my heart, for I desire to delight in your will, not just endure it
- In the same way as Jesus is worshiped in heaven, may he be worshiped in our church community
- In the same way as love abounds in heaven, may our church community be filled with love

SCRIPTURES TO MEDITATE ON

- Jesus came to do the Father's will—Jn 6:38
- Doing his will, the mark of a disciple—Mt 7:21
- Spiritual family—Mt 12:50
- Discern the will of God—Rom 12:2
- Fill us with the knowledge of your will—Col 1:9,10
- Not my will—Lk 22:42
- That none should perish—1 Tim 2:4
- Equipped to do his will—Heb 13:21

- Paul pursued God's will—Acts 21:14
- Answers to prayer—1 Jn 3:22
- Thankfulness—1 Thes 5:18
- A chosen people—1 Pt 2:4,5
- Unity of the faith—Eph 4:11-16
- That we would be one—Jn 17: 21,22
- Dwelling place of God is with man—Rev 21:3,4
- I will build my Church—Mt 16:18

GROUP DISCUSSION QUESTIONS:

1. Are there some areas where you have given up on seeing God's will (as revealed in scripture) done in your life, family, or church? Could you believe again?
2. Can you think of an experience where God's timing ended up being much better than the timing you hoped for?
3. Is the practice of discerning the specific will of God for decisions in your life something you are comfortable with and confident in?

Chapter Seven

GIVE US THIS DAY

Leaving behind the opening of the three God-ward requests, we come to a petition which is a bridge into the more earthly requests. Yet, "Give us this day our daily bread" keeps a foot in both realms. Here, we bring to the Father our needs as children, be they practical, spiritual, emotional, or a combination of all three. Before we ask, he knows what we need, so there is no requirement to ask perfectly or precisely. He's a good Father who can interpret our tears or our emotional, jumbled rants; he understands what is deep in our hearts when all we can find are words of anger, frustration or pain.

Just as a natural father or mother would be able to tell you what their child means, for they can read the expressions, the body language, the tone of voice and know intimately the heart behind the words, our good Father is able to perfectly understand. With this in mind, he invites us to pray from our hearts.

Don't forget the context of this prayer. "Give us this day our daily bread," is a petition that connects asking the Father for our personal needs to the teaching of Luke 11. The same words, "give us" are used and the image of bread is repeated. The Lord is strongly emphasizing his willingness to give us what we need. He reveals this willingness through the parable of the friend at midnight in Luke 11: 5-8, through the exhortation to "ask, and it will be given you," in Luke 11:9 and through the illustration of the Good Father, giving his children both physical and spiritual food in Luke 11:11-13. In fact, when we look at the illustration of the Good Father in Matthew 7:9, Jesus says that if we ask for bread, we will not be given a stone; he makes it undeniably clear that he expects us to ask for daily bread and that he's absolutely committed to respond.

DAILY

Another notable feature of this petition is its focus on time. The only two mentions of time in the Lord's Prayer are both found here: this day and daily bread. This focus highlights both the urgency of the need and the reality that it keeps being a need, every day. In this petition we are asking that the need be met today; we can't wait or delay, there is an immediate need for bread.

A higher level of faith is required to ask that the spiritual and physical bread that we need be provided for us now, not at a distant time in the future. Everyone knows it's easier to pray for something to be granted someday, than for us to contend for it in our immediate, daily life. But in this petition, we are being invited, after the grandeur of, "On earth as it is in heaven" to believe for a very real manifestation of heaven (or heaven's provision) to enter our earthly day. With this bridging petition, we are asking for our daily portion of heaven to come to earth.

As well as urgency, the request for daily bread communicates profound dependence. We are not asking for weekly bread, something we could manage and portion out for ourselves; we are positioning ourselves in absolute dependence on God for all that we need to thrive and advance the kingdom today. Every day is purposeful, every day needs God. Jesus modelled this lifestyle of radical dependence for us. He also taught us that our walk is meant to be one of abiding and drawing everything from him as our true source.[62] He explained that apart from

---

62 Jn 15

him, we can do nothing, meaning that all fruitfulness requires drawing life from him in continual communion and dependence.[63]

However, when we ask for this heavenly bread and pray with urgency, recognizing that we need it daily, what specifically are we asking for? We need to understand this, so we will know if our prayer has been answered or if we are to keep on asking. We need to know what to believe for with fully activated faith. What then, is our bread?

BREAD, DAILY PROVISION

There is the obvious application of this request, namely, the provision of practical needs, including food, housing, clothing, transportation and other costs of living. It's a request for provision for all that we need to live, to thrive, to fulfill our callings and the vision God has for our lives. Our Father is not stingy or mean-spirited; he is profoundly generous. He is not restrained in his ability to provide by our situation, the people we know, our skills or the opportunities that may or may not surround us. As our good Father, he is not only aware of and committed to care for every need, but he also delights in our dependence on him, never expecting us to grow out of it.

At times we may think of God's provision and assume it must come as a financial gift from a benefactor, but God also provides by giving us work, by reducing our expenses and by stretching our dollars. His goal is not to make us wealthy, but to make us fruitful. If financial lack is authentically holding us back from being fruitful in our calling, it's time to exercise faith and ask boldly for what we need. Bear in mind it is God's name we want made famous, his kingdom we want enlarged, his will we want done, through the release of his provision, not our own.

A desire for wealth which is actually a desire for position, power, affluence or independence from God is not God's way. Paul warns us that the love of money is the root of all kinds of evil, so we must handle

63 Jn 15:4

our finances, be they abundant or not, without allowing them to capture our affections.[64]

At the same time, remember, we are not impoverished orphans. There is a commonly used statement in the Church that "God won't always give you what you want, but he gives you what you need." While there is an element of truth in this when it comes to the Lord not indulging our attraction to materialism, this statement has been used to imply that God will only ever give us survival rations and that his provision barely gets us through. Thankfully, this perception of a tightfisted God doesn't play out in scripture! Remember, whenever Jesus multiplied bread (or created wine), there was more than enough.[65]

When Paul wrote to the Philippian church, he told them the Lord had taught him how to shield his heart from the lure of money and to have contentment and peace regardless of whether he was in a time of abundance or lack.[66] This is a posture of trust and dependence on Jesus, so much so that Paul became unmoved by finances. Indeed, he declared, he could do all things through Christ who strengthened him. He could, by God's strengthening grace, walk in a way that lack didn't scare him, nor did abundance trigger independence in him.

BREAD FROM HEAVEN

After the feeding of the five thousand with more than enough bread for all, Jesus identified that the crowds were following simply to feed their bellies.[67] He admonished them, calling them to set their sights higher, to pursue bread that endures to eternal life, rather than merely food that perishes. Then he revealed that he is the Bread from Heaven, the Bread of Life. Perhaps he's saying the same thing to us today.

"Jesus then said to them, 'Truly, truly, I say to you, it was not Moses

64 1 Tim 6:10
65 Mk 6:42,43 Jn 2:6-10
66 Phil 4:11-13
67 Jn 6:26

who gave you the bread from heaven, but my Father gives you the true bread from heaven. For the bread of God is he who comes down from heaven and gives life to the world.' They said to him, 'Sir, give us this bread always.'

Jesus said to them, 'I am the bread of life; whoever comes to me shall not hunger, and whoever believes in me shall never thirst.'" Jn 6:32-35

This passage in John reveals that as we pray for our daily bread, more than anything, it's Jesus himself we need to feed on. Feeding on him is more than listening to him, obeying him, following him, enjoying him, worshiping him or thinking about him; it's actually daily receiving him into our hearts by faith. It's welcoming into our hearts and lives all that he is and all that he brings, so that we are filled and sustained by him.

This is a petition full of mystery and invitation into the deep things of God. Don't let it merely become a prayer for practical needs to be met, even though this is important. Remember the early Church said that the Lord's Prayer was full of mystery and power. This is one of the primary places to encounter both of these.

What you will also notice in this passage from John is the reference to manna. In Jesus's words, "it was not Moses who gave you the bread from heaven."[68] The miracle of manna is recorded in Exodus 16, a story of radical dependence on God and supernatural provision. But we may be so familiar with the story we gloss over its power. Let's take a more careful look at what was really happening.

Israel, two million strong, was journeying through the desert and found themselves without food or any means of getting food. Drawing on natural resources, they were finished. Feeding themselves was utterly impossible and their situation was dire—but God was in their midst. He himself fed them, all of them. He fed the entire nation every day with a creative miracle—making something out of nothing—for forty years. Everything they needed to nourish them, to give them strength

68 Jn 6:32

and vigour was packed into that manna. It was the food that met the need of the youngest toddlers, the protein craving young men and the most frail of the aged.

As with all cultures, eating together was the primary place of fellowship, gathering and hospitality for the Israelites. Manna provided for this need as well. For forty years this daily miracle was a sign and a wonder that Israel was never to forget. It was one of the signs that marked them as a supernatural people; as God's own possession.

In even greater ways, in the days of the Church, are we not marked as a supernatural people, with God in our midst? The Old Covenant is a shadow of the surpassing glory of the New Covenant. This petition and its reference to manna, should stir us to boldly ask for signs, wonders and miracles, even stunning creative miracles. It should provoke us to ask largely—manna fed two million people—not just once, but every day. It fed a nation. Do we have faith for miracles big enough to touch a nation? Let's stretch our faith to ask for signs and wonders!

WORD OF GOD

When Moses spoke to Israel about the reason for manna he said these famous words, which Jesus quoted: "*...Man does not live by bread alone, but by every word that comes from the mouth of God.*"[69] So clearly, this is an important application of the petition, "Give us this day our daily bread."

When Jesus quotes Deuteronomy, he is reminding us that we are not just physical creatures; we need the word of God for our spiritual life and strength, with even greater urgency than daily food. We need the scriptures and we need God to speak to us. We can say with Peter, "Lord where else could we go, for you have the words of life."[70] As we pray this prayer we can ask that the scriptures would open to us daily and we would hear God's word guiding us, encouraging us, correcting us and strengthening us.

As we pray this prayer, we may be confronted with our neglect of

---

69 Deut 8:3; Mt 4:4

70 Jn 6:68

the scriptures. Do we regularly make time to read, meditate and wait on God to speak through the Bible? Or do we assume that we already have enough exposure and familiarity with scripture to sustain us? If we don't make time to "feed", how can we, with integrity, pray to be fed? Again, we see how praying this amazing prayer gently and daily disciples us.

Jesus anticipated that many of us would struggle with consistent Bible reading and spoke directly to this issue when he taught us that if we asked the Father for bread, he would not give us a stone.[71] For some, your experience with Bible reading may have felt like it's been a heavy, lifeless weight (a stone) in your life, like a duty you were unhappily saddled with and which has never been a blessing. This can completely turn around! Ask the Father as his child for daily bread and read with a heart full of expectant faith. You will be surprised and delighted with the life that begins to spring up from the scriptures.

In times of revival there is typically a renewed love for the word of God. The scriptures come alive and suddenly become sweeter than honey, more cherished than great wealth. This can be our reality. This is the way we were meant to live: in daily, glorious communion with the Lord through his word.

In Matthew 4: 4 the Greek word for "word" is *rhema*, which means, "the now word" rather than the logos word, which would refer to a more static word. This emphasizes again that the Lord intends to speak to us and to give us spiritual life through his words. As we pray for the word of the Lord to come to our hearts we recognize that, while the scriptures are the primary and authoritative source of the word of God to us, he can speak through other means. He can speak through prophecy, visions, a sense of his leading, dreams, other believers and by many other ways. Let's stay alert and listening to the voice of God.

NOT JUST FOR US

In prayer, as we lift up this petition of "Give us this day our daily bread,"

71 Mt 7:9

we must remember that there is an "us" in this petition. Our communities need his bread. The whole dilemma in the parable of the friend at midnight was the lack of bread to give to the guest who had come from afar. This could apply to all the ways we interpret this prayer for bread. Whether we are asking for more of Jesus himself, his word, his miracles or his provision, we want to give these away, to share with the hungry around us.

One of the powerful apostolic requests for prayer that Paul penned to the Thessalonian church was a request for intercession for his work in Corinth, asking that "the word of the Lord may speed ahead and be honoured."[72] It's vital that we pray for the gospel to spread rapidly through our communities, but not just spread, that it would be received well or as Paul said, that it would be honoured.

There is much room in this petition for fervent intercession to empower fruitful preaching and teaching of the gospel. In fact, this is a prayer that reaffirms the posture of dependence upon the Lord to give us the living word for others. It is also a place to pray that that word would be so anointed it would be effective and fruitful wherever it's proclaimed, transforming many hearts. We can pray this for those that serve in pulpit ministries, but also for every Christian who daily carries the very good news of the gospel of Jesus into the world.

BREAD OF THE PRESENCE

Another important reference to bread in the Old Testament is the Bread of the Presence, a feature of the tabernacle.[73]

The Church is the New Covenant temple of God. He intends our lives to be full of his presence, to the point that we are continually refreshed, strengthened and revived. It begins with our personal walk: we choose to draw near, to be continually filled with his Spirit and presence.

---

72 2 Thes 3:1

73 Ex 25:30

Drawing near to God personally involves cultivating and honouring his presence, valuing intimacy and union with Christ in every way. Committing time to listen, wait, fellowship, worship and pray helps build our intimacy with him and increase his presence in our lives. This enables us to live like the tree planted by waters which never ceases to bear fruit, even in times of harsh drought.[74] We live drawing from a supernatural source, a supernatural river.

This presence-filled lifestyle affects those around us as well, bringing the love, peace, joy, holiness and other attributes of the kingdom of God into the spiritual climate of our homes, our neighbourhoods and workplaces. All with the purpose of revealing Jesus. The presence brings the supernatural power of the Spirit into our simple, often mundane lives first as individuals and then even more when we join together, as he promises that when two or three are gathered in his name, he would tangibly "be there in our midst."[75]

The presence of God marks us as a radically different, supernatural community. It's not just a nice bonus, it's the centrepiece, the evidence that we are his. When the presence increases to a notable level, revival breaks out, for the presence of God is always the major feature of revival.

Let's cry out daily for more of God's manifest presence in our lives and in our churches with the genuine longing and urgency that the Lord's Prayer reflects.

COMMUNION

Perhaps the place we can expect to encounter the presence of God most intensely is when we gather at the communion table. Here we give fitting honour to Jesus' sacrifice as we, in harmony with all of heaven declare, "Worthy is the Lamb who was slain!"

The Church celebrates the sacrament of communion in a wide variety of ways, even using quite different language for it, which reveals

---

74 Jer 17:8
75 Mt 18:20

our differences in theological orientation but can also exacerbate our divisions. Tragically, communion, which should be the pinnacle of our expression of unity within the Body of Christ, has become a minefield fraught with division as we hold to entrenched positions on what we believe to be the most biblical approach to this sacrament.

Still, we are all united in our desire to encounter more of God and communion is a profoundly meaningful way for that to happen. We are restoring, renewing and celebrating our union with Jesus, which should lead to us restoring, renewing, and celebrating our unity with each other.

For the early Christians, communion, or the Lord's Table, was a weekly occurrence and the apex of their worship. They expected to have encounters with Jesus and leaned into the supernatural fellowship the disciples had with Christ on the road to Emmaus (Lk 24) as a prototype of how the Lord intended to "reveal himself in the breaking of the bread."[76] Like those disciples, they expected their hearts also to be renewed and burn within them. Regardless of our denominational perspectives, we can all pray that the encounter with Jesus we experience at the communion table would become more powerful and life-changing.

In some churches, communion is infrequent. In others it's not emphasized at all, yet the power of this sacrament is real. Jesus gave it to us for revival purposes, so let's pray for the fullness of what he intended as he taught on the bread of heaven to be actualized.[77]

Scripturally, we are admonished to come to the communion table in a worthy manner.[78] What does this mean? I believe most denominations would agree that this involves repenting of all known sin and being at peace with our brothers and sisters in Christ, as much as it lies with us to do so.[79] However, the sad reality is that these two requirements are often not adhered to and there are many situations where communion is received month after month, even while members of the

---

76 Lk 24, especially verse 35

77 Jn 6:32-58

78 1 Cor 11:27-28

79 Rom 12:18

same congregation are not on speaking terms. Let's pray for this feast of communion to become the moment where ongoing division, anger and broken relationships in the Body of Christ are arrested and humbly brought to the cross. As we pray the Lord's Prayer, let's ask him that our provision of bread would include a strengthening of this place of genuine restoration, reconciliation and unity within the body of Christ.

> *"And they devoted themselves to the apostles' teaching and the fellowship, to the breaking of bread and the prayers." Acts 2:42*

> *"And day by day, attending the temple together and breaking bread in their homes, they received their food with glad and generous hearts…" Acts 2:46*

COMMUNITY

At this point of the prayer, we can ask the Father for the daily bread of healthy community and fellowship in the Body of Christ. This is not just a fluffy, optional request for nice social times that we can take or leave, there is something much more weighty here.

Mankind was made for community, not isolation. This is revealed in the scriptures but also through the universal craving for healthy, authentic community.[80] It all reveals this original design.

But we now live in a time where the family (the foundation of community), has deteriorated so dramatically that replacement for community is being sought in many, often unhealthy, ways. This is where the Church should shine, not only with building and restoring healthy families, but in walking out community beyond the family unit. We are called to community that's filled with God's love and is a safe and healing, yet a missional and maturing place to live. This is true *koinonia*: heart-level, transparent, growing relationships that knit people together in deep love, even people whose lives would never naturally intersect.

---

80 Gen 2:18

The Lord is inviting the Church into these kinds of deep relationships and communities; he's constantly seeking to knit us together in genuine love. Those that are walking this way are greatly blessed, but, the reality is that not everyone has a healthy life-giving, Christ-centred community available to them in their local church. We are a broken people, struggling with all kinds of dysfunctions and wounds that we have not yet found healing for. This means that relationships in many local churches can be stuck at an immature, surface level. Still, we long for more. Throughout the New Testament we have revelation and instructions for building community in a Jesus way, a way that is radically different from the world.

Praying for the bread of fellowship to be given to the Church is not just asking for a better social life. It's asking for Jesus' life to be expressed through our corporate life together in all the places we bump into each other, as well as the ways we celebrate each other. It's asking for his heavenly reality to infuse our earthbound humanity. It's calling for his revival life to transform our relationships.

When we look at the wide variety of biblical ways this petition can be prayed we really see a much fuller picture of what Jesus was instructing us to pray for. As with other parts of the prayer, it's always important we are led by the Spirit, not by our minds, our lists or sense of religious obligation. With this in mind, please consider these different approaches to praying "Give us this day our daily bread" as suggestions that the Holy Spirit can use to inspire you and to activate your heart in fiery prayer, rather than additional requirements to be added to your "to do" list. Remember, he gives us good, nourishing, life-giving bread when we ask, not stones.

APPLYING IT IN PRAYER

Let's look at how we can apply this petition in our personal prayer lives.

- Father, increase your presence in my life; I want to encounter you
- I pursue communion and intimate fellowship with you; as I

draw near to you, Father draw near to me

- May your holy presence be so evident on my life that it would supernaturally impact others, bringing great glory to you
- Awaken hunger in my heart that I would not be satisfied with yesterday's fellowship with you; it must be fresh for today
- As you gave manna, mark us also with daily miracles
- Grant me full provision in every area of lack
- I utterly depend on you for all my needs: financial, emotional, spiritual, relational
- Provide for the poor in my community and show me how I, and my church, can serve them well
- Deliver me from trusting in money; you are my provider, not my employer or bank account
- Train my heart to be generous and give liberally, so that I could be like you
- I need your word: speak to me from your scriptures
- I lean into you, believing you will speak a living word to my heart today
- Increase the gifts of prophecy, teaching and preaching in our church, let the word of God abound
- Encounter your people at the communion table
- May communion be holy in our church; let all receive it worthily, with clean hands, pure hearts and restored relationships
- Increase your power and presence as we take communion; may healing break out
- Build authentic, safe, Christ-centred community in our church
- Let gifts of hospitality thrive and excel in our church, that we would be knit in kingdom fellowship

SCRIPTURES TO MEDITATE ON

- Jesus, the Bread of Heaven—Jn 6:30-58
- Don't be anxious—Mt 6:25-34
- Cannot serve two masters—Mt 6:24
- No love of money—1 Tim 6:10
- Sharing within the Church—2 Cor 8:8-15
- He provides seed and bread—2 Cor 9:8-10
- Last supper—Mk 14:22
- Not by bread alone but by every word of God—Lk 4:4, Mt 4:4
- Revealed in the breaking of bread—Lk 24:35
- Early church breaking bread—Acts 2:42,46
- Communion—1 Cor 10:17
- Righteous will not be forsaken—Ps 37:25
- Share your bread with the hungry—Isa 58:7
- In as much as you give to others—Mt 25:37
- Manna—Ex 16:12-21
- More than necessary food—Job 23:12
- Freely receive—Isa 55:2
- The Lord our Provider—Gen 22:14
- The Bread of the Presence—Ex 25:30

GROUP DISCUSSION QUESTIONS:

1. If you struggle with either the fear of lack, or the love of money, how could understanding the goodness of the Father change that?
2. Has this chapter given you some new ways to pray "Give us this day our daily bread"? Which of these seems most important to you right now?
3. How does daily dependence on the Father challenge your natural independence?

Chapter Eight

FORGIVE US

As we draw close to God and invite more of his presence into our daily life, he responds. He draws near and his nearness brings a sudden awareness of his holiness. This is what Isaiah experienced in his encounter with God and it triggered a cry of "Woe is me, for I am unclean."[81] Repentance is not an outdated Old Testament concept, even though in today's world it is seen as highly unpopular. Jesus in his wisdom knew that, "Forgive us our sins" was a prayer that we needed to be instructed to pray and it would need to be prayed often.

But the order of the petitions and where in the prayer he sets this request for forgiveness really matters. It reveals his true understanding of human nature. Many of us would leave "Forgive us our sins" out completely when crafting this prayer, while others would set it as the opening of the prayer. Neither of these were what Jesus chose. Jesus instructs us to pray for daily bread before we move into asking for forgiveness and this reveals his heart.

It's human nature to attempt to earn our blessings and our salvation. We are hard-wired towards the independence of self-salvation, self-provision and self-protection. We seek to work at what is needed

81 Isa 6 especially verse 5

to achieve a spiritual end. But all progress in the kingdom is through Christ, with us believing in him and receiving grace from him. It's not just salvation, but all of the kingdom that is received by faith through grace. Not by works. This is a truth that continually challenges, humbles and offends us.

We have been journeying through this prayer, step by step, petition by petition. We've just spent time asking for daily bread, a request that involves leaning into all the beautiful benefits of intimate communion with him, but now we ask for cleansing. If the order were to be reversed, it would reinforce our assumption that we have to get cleaned up before we could receive the blessings of his presence or provision. We'd jump to the conclusion that we had to earn access first. Instead, like the father in the story of the prodigal son, our Father embraces us *before* he cleans us up and robes us.[82] The embrace and welcome come first.

However, the call to cleansing is not optional. We mustn't stop at receiving daily bread; we must continue on into living in the exhilaration of a freshly cleansed heart. As we do, we're very aware that we are speaking to the Father, not just a generic "God", but the Father who has revealed his immense kindness to us, as we saw in the chapter on Our Father.

Jesus helps us to be real and transparent with the Father who loves us so deeply. Real, even to the point of being honest about our need for cleansing. So often we, like Adam, hide or mask parts of our lives because of shame. At other times, we will be defensive or attempt to shift the blame like our first forefather did. The Lord helps us to face our need for cleansing squarely, as the words of the prayer are "Forgive us our trespasses" (or in other versions, "Forgive us our sins") rather than, "Forgive us our sins, *if* we have sinned." There is no "if." There is a presumption that we *have* sinned and thus need to receive forgiveness, cleansing and restoration from God. Lovingly, Jesus recognizes that we don't naturally humble ourselves in repentance, so he helps us take the first step. This petition of repentance reveals that Jesus knows we have

---

82 Lk 15:11-32

sinned and he's urging us to bring our sins to the light. He gives us freedom to be real and fully confess what we might otherwise have glossed over or hidden.

If we start from the presumption that we likely need repentance, we are positioned to listen carefully to the conviction of the Holy Spirit who would show us words, deeds, internal words, attitudes, thoughts or motives that grieve him. He can also bring to light sins of omission, things that we haven't done that he instructed us to do. These could include lack of love, mercy, faith and so on. These kinds of sins also grieve him.

Praying this prayer daily gives time and space for the Lord to address these sins and lead us into a heartfelt repentance. It's important to remember however, that the Holy Spirit is the one who convicts and the one who sanctifies. We mustn't critically scrutinize our own lives, but rather trust the Holy Spirit's conviction to lead us to repentance. At the same time, the accuser, the devil, may try to find an opportunity to condemn and shame us. His voice more typically attacks our identity and leaves us feeling worthless, condemned and even hopeless. He rarely identifies a specific sin but declares a hopeless accusation over our life. By contrast, the Holy Spirit shows us exactly where we have stumbled and beckons us to bring this sin to the cross so we can be set free. Leading us into life and renewed hope.

Because we are cultivating dependence on Christ, rather than independence from him, coming to him daily for cleansing is not a sign of weakness or failure, but a recognition of the reality of our need. We don't grow out of our need for repentance even as we mature in him. Although there may not be as many overt issues of blatantly sinful words or deeds, because we make this a part of our daily prayer, it gives an opportunity for the Lord to begin to highlight deeper attitudes, heart postures and motives. We pray: "Search me, O God, and know my heart: try me, and know my thoughts: and see if there be any wicked way *in* me."[83]

---

83 Ps 139:23-24b KJV

This daily practice of coming to the cross in repentance and seeking forgiveness builds in us a wholesome lifestyle of keeping short accounts with God and others. It means that thoughts and attitudes are arrested before developing into entrenched sins. It gives an opportunity for the Holy Spirit to redirect us, correct us and restore us to a right spirit every day, nipping in the bud the progression of sin: guilt, alienation from God, shame and then hiding. Sin in the Christian's life, if left unaddressed, brings "the wages of death" through things like hardened hearts, double lives, lack of peace and a generally backslidden state.[84] If instead, we faithfully come to the Father and ask him to show us what might grieve him, we won't drift farther away or live under a niggling sense of undefined shame. We live daily in the confidence, joy and glory of a newly-washed heart. We are also filled with a greater revelation and deeper adoration of Jesus because of the reality of "He who is forgiven much loves much."[85] If you want to love Jesus more, this is one of the most powerful ways for that love to grow in your life.

When we pray "Forgive us our sins", the Lord immediately responds but as we draw near to the cross, there are some other features of this cleansing and redeeming that we should be aware of so that its work authentically transforms us. Asking for forgiveness includes confession, sorrow over sin (contrition), genuine repentance, receiving both forgiveness and cleansing, restoration, as well as possibly confession, apologies or restitution to others. Let's look at these different steps in a bit more depth.

Confession

A confession that is humble and honest takes full responsibility for our part in the sin. It doesn't make excuses or blame others. It uses clear, strong language which doesn't minimize or deflect the guilt of what we've done. Calling our sin "mistakes", "wrong choices," or "places where we need healing" isn't true confession. It's squirming out of the look-me-in-the-eyes

84 Rom 6:23
85 Lu 7:47

conviction that the Holy Spirit is graciously giving. Conviction must be received as a gift, not resisted or diffused with our defensive excuses.

Sorrow

It's so important to be genuinely sorry for what our sin has done to God and others. We can't just be sorry that our sin came to the light or sorry because of the negative consequences it has brought. We need to hate our sin the way God does. Not hate ourselves—our sin. Declare war on your sin, refuse to give it an inch of your affections! If this seems like a foreign concept, ask the Lord to change your heart to love holiness the way he does, as this will also align you with his emotions towards sin. But thanks be to God, no matter how deeply we have sinned, it still does not define us; it is not our identity.

Repentance

The concept of repentance is that we turn around and go the opposite direction. But when we teach this practice without including the necessity of confession and sorrow for sin, we make it seem like we've simply turned down the wrong street and need to do a U-turn to get back on track to our destination. Making a wrong turn when we drive has no emotional impact; our heart isn't involved in any way, but with authentic repentance it is. Strong's Concordance defines the word in Greek (*metanoia)* this way: "to change one's mind for better, heartily to amend with abhorrence of one's past sins." Bible scholar, F.F. Bruce brings further light to this concept with his thoughts: "Repentance involves a turning with contrition from sin to God; the repentant sinner is in the proper condition to accept the divine forgiveness."[86]

Receiving forgiveness

This is the step where having humbly asked for God's mercy, we simply

86 F. F. Bruce. *The Acts of the Apostles* (London: Tyndale, 1952, p. 97).

receive it by faith. We stand in the promise that "*If we say we have no sin, we deceive ourselves, and the truth is not in us. If we confess our sins, he is faithful and just to forgive us our sins and to cleanse us from all unrighteousness.*"[87] We trust the Lord to forgive us and to cast our sins into the sea, so they will never be brought up or held against us in any way.[88]

This is the stage where we have to follow his lead and forgive ourselves if we are struggling with this. We cannot refuse to forgive ourselves if God, who is perfectly holy and righteous, has determined we are forgiven.

Receiving cleansing

Like forgiveness, we receive a full and complete cleansing by faith. We receive the washing of his blood, able to make all our filthiness and all that we are ashamed of exquisitely clean and perfectly new. Once we have asked for forgiveness and cleansing, we must refuse to give room to the enemy's accusations that are intent on keeping us emotionally locked into feelings of unworthiness. We stand on the truth of the power of the blood and so letting go of all shame, we fully embrace the gift of a washed heart, soul and life.

Mindsets of shame that have their roots in our history may need some additional ministry and healing, but it is vital to know the Father has never intended his children to live in shame. If there is shame in our lives because of unconfessed sin, let's get it cleaned up! If there is shame because of past wounding or lies we have believed, let's get ministry and healing. Living in shame will never produce in us the kind of healthy, joyous life which Jesus paid for.

Refilling

Once we've received cleansing, we ask the Holy Spirit to fill us afresh.

---

87 1 Jn 1:8-9
88 Mic 7:19

He is holy and will lift his presence, in a measure, from our lives, if we are walking in known sin. But when we repent, ask for forgiveness and cleansing, he is delighted to refill us. The Spirit will again rest upon our lives and draw us into a renewed, joyful fellowship and communion.[89] Then as we are refilled, we are empowered to walk in greater holiness and all the fruits of the Spirit.

Being reconciled to others

At times, our sin has impacted others in a way that we need to express our repentance to them as well. The steps are the same: an authentic confession where we take full responsibility for our wrong doing, humbly expressing sorrow and repentance, then finally, a request for forgiveness.

In some situations, restitution is appropriate. If you stole something, return it. If you damaged something through your neglect, pay for it to be fixed.

Fruits of repentance

Finally, the evidence of true repentance is a change. We naturally show forth the fruit of repentance by doing things differently, thinking differently and hating sin instead of accommodating it.

The change might be very slow and you might fall again in the same place a hundred times or more, but each time, as you repent, you take steps towards permanent change. This change, once fully established in our lives, blooms into transformation. Jesus is not just the One who forgives us for our sin, he actually delivers us from sin and its slavery. He is the Lamb of God who *takes away* the sin of the world.[90] If you are not seeing change, seek out a qualified Christian counsellor or a pastor and consider with them what is holding you back from freedom in this area of your life.

---

89 Ps 51:10-12
90 Jn 1:29

James tells us bluntly that we deceive ourselves if we assert we have faith and our lives don't show the fruit of it. His words are, "Faith without works is dead."[91] In the same way, as we repent, Jesus expects us to genuinely bear the fruit of that change of heart and mind in our lives.[92]

OTHER FRUITS OF REPENTANCE

Regularly following the Spirit's lead into repentance truly does lead us into transformation, but there are other types of glorious, kingdom fruit that spring up as well.

One of the most striking is a heightened tenderness to the Holy Spirit's conviction. It is the goodness of God that leads us to repentance by the convicting work of the Spirit in our lives.[93] Conviction puts us in touch with our guilt while revealing, in contrast, the Lord's holiness. It's not fun, but oh, so necessary.

Were God to only pour blessings into our lives without ever disciplining us, we would never be set free from sin. We would never experience deep sorrow for sin, have our lives trained in righteousness or enjoy the wonder of transformation. In His kindness he knows we need the cross and brings us there for redemption and life. This is such breathtaking goodness.

After repentance, conviction continues to minister to our hearts, as it becomes the grace of the fear of the Lord. Because of authentic contrition over the sin and our change of mind and heart towards it (repentance), we now hate what we once condoned. The fear of the Lord combined with our new perspective of this sin become mighty deterrents, protecting us from carelessly falling into it again. Of course, there's no guarantee that we won't, but these certainly act as speed bumps and slow us down!

---

91 Jas 2:20
92 Mt 3:8
93 Rom 2:4

WALKING IN THE LIGHT

A lifestyle of walking in the light becomes a reality when we quickly and frequently repent; when we pray this petition daily. As well as a heightened tenderness to conviction, we notice if the Spirit has withdrawn slightly from our lives. We notice the moment he may be grieved with something we've said or done or an attitude that has risen in our hearts. Right then, we can turn and be restored again.

This responsiveness to conviction means we don't go for weeks and months, aware that the Holy Spirit is no longer tangibly present in our lives, but uncertain as to why he has retreated. It means that we take the time to ask him to show us what has caused his presence to lift off of our lives in a measure; we're unwilling to just plow ahead, living without his daily nearness.

Revival comes when God draws near and his nearness changes everything in our lives and communities. Cultivating his nearness requires that we grow in genuinely honouring the Holy Spirit through sensitivity, humility and being quick to repent. We draw near to him and he keeps drawing nearer to us.[94]

This lifestyle of walking in closeness and sensitivity to the Holy Spirit means his nearness fills us with boldness, confidence and joy that won't stop bubbling up. It was this glorious presence that enabled the early disciples to live in such astonishing ways.

HUMILITY

Another major area of fruit that comes from praying the Lord's Prayer, and particularly this ongoing request for forgiveness, is that we stay aware of our frailty and our susceptibility towards stumbling into sin. This reality grounds us in humility and leads to transparent, openly vulnerable relationships, so essential for true community. As we embrace the cross by praying this petition of repentance, it dismantles our pride

94 Jas 4:8

and self-righteousness and as we do it daily, a beautiful, meek and tender heart is the result.

Praying this way and embracing authentic humility enables us to easily flow in compassion and mercy towards those who are likewise stumbling, even in much more extreme ways. Our natural tendency towards self-righteousness and the judgment of others is kept in check. Jesus illustrated this tendency when he gave us the parable of the pharisee and the tax collector.[95] Thankfully, as we grow in grace-filled humility, the realization of "there, but for the grace of God, go I" rises up as we witness depraved displays of wickedness.

KEY TO REVIVAL

In a very tangible way, "Forgive us our sins" is a stunningly powerful prayer for revival. Imagine for a moment the entire Church across denominations and nations praying this prayer—earnestly, humbly and daily—praying it and really meaning it.

This alone would be like the shock of Jesus overturning the tables in the temple, with animals and coins scattering in all directions! Decades of entrenched sin, compromise with the world and self-centered living would be overturned by a revival of true holiness. The Church would emerge from living double lives where fear, shame and doubt drive us into camouflaging who we really are. We would emerge and step into the peace, power and mission of God. Cultural Christianity would be upgraded to the genuine, radical New Testament lifestyle which once turned the world upside down. This is the lifestyle of revival.

This is actually where God is going. Jesus will have a glorious Church; his spotless Bride.[96] It's not just his desire, it's his plan and he is able to accomplish it. In this prayer Jesus invites us to take steps toward this vision, to partner with him in speeding its fulfillment. Praying this prayer daily soon establishes us in this lifestyle of drawing near

95 Lk 18:9-14
96 Eph 5:27

to God, welcoming the work of repentance and the revival it brings into our hearts. Happily, we also discover that although it begins with us, it doesn't just stay with us!

THIS IS CORPORATE

Up until now we have only looked at this part of the prayer with a personal application. Really, we've been considering it as if it was "Forgive me my sins" and while this is exactly where we need to start—with our own hearts, we also need to pray it as fully as Jesus gave it to us, "Forgive us *our* sins."

The corporate nature of this prayer is a call to turn away from the Western individualism that has so permeated our worldview. We have been accustomed to privacy and individualism, especially when it comes to repentance and confession, to the point that for most, the corporate language of this prayer is unsettling. But Jesus is providing us an opportunity to choose community and transparency, to be willing to confess our sins one to another and pray for each other, rather than keep the true nature of our struggles secret.[97] Jesus is inviting us into disclosing our sins, not to shame us, but to bring us into a wonderful victory, a victory that is much harder to gain if we struggle alone. Opening our hearts in confession does however, require an appropriate setting with someone who is trustworthy and mature, or it becomes unsafe. But the need for a high standard of maturity for a safe confession is not a reason to avoid it. Instead, let's build churches where there is not only a place for confession, but where confession is a normal part of our lives. Building in this way creates a strong and holy community.

Corporate confession can also be done, with moments of silence provided for this purpose in our services or prayer meetings. Building this into our corporate meetings reaffirms the importance of this practice and reminds us that none of us are entirely sanctified yet.

Another application of this petition is asking the Father for

97 Jas 5:16

forgiveness on behalf of others, particularly on behalf of "our people." This involves stepping into the role of a spokesperson and is especially effective if we are already hold a position of authority. The effectiveness is even greater if those that we speak on behalf of are united and carry the same heart of repentance. A good example would be a pastor repenting on behalf of their congregation that has fallen into a sin. It becomes an entirely different thing, however, if you seek to repent on behalf of a city, a region, your ethnicity or a nation. It is unlikely the majority of the people you are speaking for are united in agreement with your repentance. It's more likely most are not following God at all, so your voice is not their voice. Repentance can't be papered over unwilling hearts; the Lord never overrides our will, but rather honours our choices. It's important that we don't attempt to wield dominion where we don't actually have it—over the will and choices of others.

When considering our communities and cities, I'd suggest that a better way to pray is to intercede fervently that there would be widespread receptivity and responsiveness to the conviction of God. This would *bring* a heartfelt, corporate cry of "Forgive us our sins," as altars are filled and revival breaks out.

Our communities are generally so sin-saturated and hardened to the fear of the Lord that real intercession is desperately needed to change this. We need intercession that contends for hearts to be softened and awakened, because only then will we see a widespread response of true repentance.

Charles Finney, the great American revivalist, based his prayers and preaching on the principle that individuals and even communities as a whole, were in varying stages of being awakened, becoming ripe for revival.[98] The initial stage he called being a Careless Sinner, having no care or concern for God. For these ones, God rarely, if ever, even enters their thoughts.

---

98 Charles Finney (1792-1875). For more on Finney's prayer and evangelism methods: Charles G. Finney, *Revival Lectures* (Old Tappan, New Jersey: Fleming H. Revell Company Publishers)

In our day, this would describe those who feel no need for God, whether they are at the pinnacle of success in life or destitute, broken and addicted. They are not looking to the spiritual world to help their lives in any way and God is irrelevant to them. Most of our nation lives in this state of Careless Sinner.

The second group would be those that are Awakened Sinners. This is the group that is aware of God, they are seekers, aware there are spiritual dynamics to life, but don't yet see their need for Christ. They may even sense that God is pursuing them. They may have supernatural dreams or unusual "coincidences" happening in their lives which reveal God's love reaching out to them. It could be that they run into an old neighbour who now has a wonderful testimony. These ones are aware that something is wooing them towards Jesus.

The last group is the Convicted Sinners, who are not just awakened, but are very conscious of their need for the Lord while still resisting him. This group is in the midst of a continual wrestle in their hearts, feeling one minute as though they want God, then the next being repelled by the cost and the offence of the cross. They are the ones trekking the shadowy slopes of the valley of decision.[99]

Finney's perspective was that the primary way people moved through these groups and fully yielded to Christ was through intercessory prayer on their behalf. His partner in ministry, Father Nash, would go ahead to the site of a planned preaching crusade to "break up the fallow ground." This would involve deep intercession for the people of the region to shift from being Careless or Awakened Sinners to desiring Christ at any cost. Finney's astonishing success as a revivalist was by in large because of this ministry of intercession.

Today, while we live in different times (even the names Finney used to describe these groups of unbelievers seems offensive), the principle of wooing and preparing hearts for the gospel is the same. More than anything, it is the work of prayer that moves hearts from being indifferent to God to running earnestly towards him. It could be a change that

99 Joel 3:14

happens very quickly or it could take place over many years, but the source of change is the same. It's the work of conviction and drawing by the Holy Spirit, a work that is activated and sustained by faithful, fervent prayer.

What if we prayed for our communities and cities, even for our nation, like Father Nash did! Fervent intercession for a great, national awakening of our need for Jesus, an awakening to the degree that the prayer of "Forgive us our sins" would break out on a massive scale, (as it has always done in seasons of revival). If we prayed, would not the same God who heard Father Nash's prayers hear ours?

"Forgive us our sins" is a petition that can change everything for us as we agree with Jesus that we need regular, even daily washing from all the ways that sin hides in our lives and motives. It's also a prayer of deep intercession for the Body of Christ to encounter the awesome holiness of God, which will set us free from living double lives full of guilt and shame.

Finally, it is a prayer for a great awakening in our communities, cities and nations. It is a prayer that can change history. "Forgive us our sins."

APPLYING IT IN PRAYER

As with the previous petitions, here are some suggestions for ways you could consider praying this one.

- I repent for ______, forgive me, wash me
- Father show me where you are grieved with my attitudes, motives, lifestyle or words
- Help me to stand in your light and not hide from you or reject your conviction
- Grant me a love for holiness
- Let me see sin the way you see it, with holy hatred

- As you forgive me and cleanse me, I receive this forgiveness and forgive myself
- Fill me with your Spirit afresh, that I would be empowered to walk in your holiness
- May a new longing of holiness awaken in my church
- Anoint the preaching of the gospel to bring freedom to those enslaved by secret sin
- Grant us more of the fear of the Lord
- Reveal Jesus as the One who goes beyond forgiving sin to taking it away from us
- Forgive us our sins, as a church, in the ways we have stumbled and grieved you
- May repentance in my church be grace filled, leading to life and fruit
- Move upon "Careless Sinners" in my life, awaken in them a sense of need for you
- Let my entire region be awakened with a new awareness and hunger for God
- Teach us, as your people, to respond well to those you are drawing to faith
- Let those who have heard of you and turned away because they thought you were exacting and harsh, now be touched by your grace
- May prodigals hear the gospel with fresh ears and may it bring hope to their hearts

SCRIPTURES TO MEDITATE ON

- Create in me a clean heart—Ps 51:9-11
- New heart—Eze 36:25-29

- Righteousness from God—Phil 3:9
- Draw near to God—Jas 4:8-10
- Times of refreshing—Acts 3:19,20
- In Christ—1 Cor 1:30
- If we claim to be without sin—1 Jn 1:8-10
- He who is forgiven much—Lk 7:47
- Be zealous and repent—Rev 3:17-20
- Save to the uttermost—Heb 7:25
- Without spot or wrinkle—Rev 19:8
- O Lord, hear—Dan 9:18, 19
- Cast into the sea—Mic 7:19
- Prodigal son—Lk 15:18-22
- With you there is forgiveness—Ps 130:3,4
- Turn from wicked ways—2 Chron 7:14
- Blessed is the man—Ps 32:1

GROUP DISCUSSION QUESTIONS:

1. What are some of the ways that keeping short accounts with God would bring more health to your emotional, spiritual or family life?
2. Does the idea of holiness seem positive or negative to you? Why?
3. Which of the different steps of asking for forgiveness (eg. confession, sorrow, repentance) has the Lord helped you to do well? Which do you want to grow in?

Chapter Nine

WE ALSO FORGIVE

The second half of the request for forgiveness is a radical, counter-culture statement rather than another petition. It's a declaration that we have already forgiven those who have sinned against us. It's proclaiming that we have wholeheartedly obeyed the Lord's unequivocal instruction to be a people who, like him, are shockingly generous with forgiveness. We pray, "Forgive us our sins, as we forgive those who have sinned against us". As we do, we are declaring that as he has forgiven, we also forgive.

When we looked at the first three petitions, we saw that they are a response to the First Commandment, to love God with all our heart, soul and mind.[100] Then as we dug deeper into the petitions of "Your kingdom come, your will be done," we saw that they are a prayerful response to the "go" in the Great Commission.[101] Now, as we consider this declaration that we have forgiven, we see the place in the prayer where the Second Commandment shines through the most brightly.[102] We are actually loving our neighbour as our self. If we truly follow this commandment to love to this degree, generous and wholehearted

---

100 Mt 22:38
101 Mt 28:18-20
102 Mt 22:39

forgiveness no longer seems like an unreasonable demand, for it's what love does.

This kind of love is foreign to our society, so there is an expectation that some measure of unforgiveness will be found in all of us. We presume that the wounds of life will leave us with experiences and relationships that we don't have the inclination or emotional capacity to forgive. Humanly speaking, this is too difficult, so we excuse ourselves and excuse each other.

But for a Christian, forgiving quickly and freely is a sign of our new birth. It's a sign of the infilling of the Spirit and his love pouring out through our lives. Who can forgive like this?! It's supernatural! The forgiveness that flows from our hearts testifies to the transforming power of the forgiveness we have received. We have been forgiven innumerable sins at the highest imaginable cost and our hearts are astonished and overwhelmed with gratitude.

Baptist theologian John Stott comments on the humility of receiving forgiveness and how it tenderizes our hearts, "God forgives only the penitent, and one of the chief evidences of true penitence is a forgiving spirit."[103]

What the prayer is reinforcing is that as Christians, we are called to live a lifestyle of loving forgiveness, day in and day out. This means that right in the moment, in the midst of the sin being committed against us—we forgive. Our posture is already love, so forgiveness is quickly offered, rather than being pried from our hearts years after the offence. This was what was taught and modelled by Jesus in the most incredible display of forgiveness, spoken from the cross, "Father, forgive them, they know not what they do."[104] It was certainly the standard that the early Church sought to follow and because the Jewish leaders, Roman government and pagan society around them were all hostile to Christianity, they had many opportunities, perhaps daily, to forgive.

---

103 John R. W. Stott, *Christian Counter-culture: The Message of the Sermon on the Mount* (Downers Grove, Ill.: InterVarsity Press, 1978),149.
104 Lk 23:34

THE EARLY CHURCH

As we follow the stories of the Apostles through the Book of Acts and the epistles we learn that they experienced martyrdoms, imprisonments, severe beatings, lashes, rejection and mocking. At times the Christians had their possessions seized and were excluded from vocational opportunities because of their faith. But in this hostile environment, the Church overcame their enemies with an unexpected weapon, their love and generous forgiveness.

A couple of examples jump out. Let's look more closely at these.

Stephen, the young deacon, was a fiery preacher. The record of his ministry begins in Acts 6, where the account tells us that he was full of faith and the Holy Spirit. A bit later it records that he was filled with grace and power, doing great wonders and signs among the people.[105] Those that opposed the Church rose up and brought Stephen before the council of the high priest. Stephen brought a defence in the form of a powerful sermon which culminated with intense conviction of the Holy Spirit coming upon all the hearers. So strong was the conviction that they ground their teeth in rage, then lashing out, stoned him to death.

But Stephen, in the last moments of his life, did what he had trained his heart to do repeatedly: he loved his enemies. Filled with the power of the Spirit, he forgave them and prayed that the Lord would also grant them forgiveness. Love and radical forgiveness were on display for all to see! Who could forgive like this? Why would he have done it?

Jesus set this forgiveness in motion from the cross and Stephen was following closely this beautiful example. Like the other early disciples, he expected that the Jesus way of continual, generous forgiveness would be the path they would follow. Another factor in Stephen's remarkable response was that he had been ordained a deacon, a significant leadership role, so he was serving the Church by courageously demonstrating forgiveness, even in this extreme setting. He was following Christ and discipling the Church at the same time.

---

105 Acts 6:8

This level of forgiveness in the face of outrageous injustice was something that none of the Jewish leaders had seen before and it was a true reflection of the nature of Christ. In Israel's history, it had only ever been God who had demonstrated this level of mercy, but now his love and forgiveness was manifesting and marking the lives of the early believers.

Paul was another example of the forgiveness that flowed in the early Church. Consider for a moment, his missionary journey to Philippi, likely in the summer of AD 51. Paul and his ministry partner, Silas, had been unjustly accused and instead of receiving a proper trial, they were stripped and beaten severely with rods, then handed over to the jailer to be imprisoned. But the jailer, most probably a retired Roman soldier with a sadistic bent, chose the worst possible cell for Paul and Silas, the inner cell with no ventilation, in the blistering Macedonian summer. In those days, the Mediterranean prisons were built with no concern for the health of the prisoners, just their security, so prisoners at times suffocated in the stifling heat and dreadful ventilation.[106]

Not only did the jailer choose the worst and darkest cell, but then secured their ankles in stocks. The Romans didn't just use stocks as additional security for their prisoners; they intended stocks to be cruel, painfully holding body parts in unnatural positions so they would cramp. Still Paul and Silas responded with forgiveness and joy. Their worship and prayer (perhaps for the jailer?) rose in the middle of the night, heartily and loudly enough to keep the whole prison awake! Then, when God sent a miraculous earthquake, instead of escaping, they chose to stay, even making sure the other prisoners did as well. Why? So that the jailer wouldn't be punished.

This was a dramatic example of loving your enemies, which along with the supernatural earthquake, convinced the jailer and his whole household of God's love and power. He was transformed by this love to

---

106 For more details of the persecutions the early Church faced: Bryan Litfin, *Getting to Know the Church Fathers: an Evangelical Introduction* (Grand Rapids: Baker Academic Publishing, 2007).

the point that this once brutal and hardened man becomes tender, kind, and attentive to Paul and Silas's needs. If Paul and Silas hadn't forgiven, this story would have ended differently. They wouldn't have had the grace to pray for the jailer, nor to stay when the earthquake occurred, which enabled them to preach to the whole family, proclaiming the love and forgiveness of Christ.

Stephen, Paul and Silas demonstrated the forgiveness and love for enemies that Jesus taught. Theirs and dozens of other examples from the New Testament illustrates that this was indeed the lifestyle which the early Church was earnestly committed to. They were real men and women facing betrayals, injustices, wicked and brutal adversaries, even grave sins within their ranks. They would have had to wrestle with their hearts to forgive; they were not superhuman. However, this standard of forgiveness meant when they prayed, "Forgive us as we forgive those who have sinned against us," it was authentic and it kept them full of the Spirit. This was an important reason the early Church so frequently saw the Spirit moving in supernatural, even revival ways.

Paul was one of the primary leaders of the Church and even though he had been their persecutor and an advocate for Stephen's stoning, there is no record of any lingering bitterness held against him. I wonder if this would be the case today. It certainly seems to be that we have drifted far from this glorious standard of grace and have a great need of spiritual renewal in this area of our lives.

NO WIGGLE ROOM

We can see that praying, "… as we forgive those who have sinned against us" identifies a tremendous need in the Church for revival, a need to return to the biblical standard of love, mercy and grace. If we cannot pray this phrase with genuine sincerity because unforgiveness lingers, the prayer arrests us and confronts us with this requirement, this glaring need in our heart. Jesus, in his wisdom, gives us no wiggle room, no way of avoiding this requirement to forgive as we pray the Lord's Prayer daily.

If he *had* left us any wiggle room, human nature is such that we would grab it with both hands! So, not only does he make it clear that we must forgive anyone who sin against us, but he clarifies the quality of that forgiveness, lest we modify it to accommodate our propensity towards unforgiveness. He instructs us to pray, "…forgive us *as* we forgive!" The "as" in the text of the prayer means that we are asking to be forgiven in the very same way, with the same quality that we have forgiven others.

Let's pursue a forgiving spirit which reaches to replicate the beauty of the Father's forgiveness, extended to us so, so many times. This is a forgiveness that is immediate (not released slowly and begrudgingly), that is full and that casts our sins into the sea where they are never brought up or used to shame us. It cannot be earned but comes by mercy and grace alone. Let's seek to forgive in the same immediate, full and free way that we've been forgiven.

In the same way that we receive grace upon grace to forgive our sin, great grace is available to us to forgive those who sin against us. It's not easy and is perhaps one of the hardest things we have to do, but grace is there. The greatness of the grace that forgives us again and again is available to empower us to be a conduit of his forgiveness.

If forgiving others seems like an insurmountable hurdle, stacked up against the pain of your experiences, I want to invite you to earnestly choose forgiveness and put your whole trust in Jesus to empower that choice with his supernatural grace. It might require a lengthy process of choosing to forgive again and again as the emotions of anger and wounding rise in your heart, but he will empower you to fully forgive, to love your neighbor as yourself. You will know this process is complete when you find the inclination of your heart is a desire for the person to be blessed, rather than to suffer God's judgement. Remember, the Lord forgives hundreds of millions, if not billions of sins *daily* as his people ask for forgiveness and new believers come to Christ asking for a lifetime of sin to be forgiven. This is what he does. He does it gladly. Let's choose to reflect that same heart and join him in this ministry.

WHO TO FORGIVE

Instead of painful offenses committed against us which we still to need to forgive, we may find that when we pray these words: "...as we forgive those who have sinned against us," nothing immediately comes to mind. But instead of assuming all is well and hurrying on to the rest of the prayer, allow the Father time to speak. He may reach back into the story of our life and remind us of a person, a situation or a wound that has faded from our immediate memory, where we never actually forgave. This gives us an opportunity to release generous, open-handed forgiveness to that person and to make sure that unforgiveness hasn't found a place to hide in our past. It could be that we did forgive but a deeper level is required. It might even be that recalling the offense that was once forgiven has triggered anger and the initial forgiveness has evaporated, leaving us to nurse a bitter grievance. If so, it's time to reinstate forgiveness and refuse to give bitterness a home in our hearts.

Allow the Lord to search your heart. Unforgiveness doesn't have to be towards a person that we have direct relationship with, it could be the personnel manager of the large company we once worked for who unjustly laid us off, a professor who gave us a failing grade, or a politician who put unbiblical laws in place. A frequent place where unforgiveness or even bitterness can remain in the heart of a Christian is a church or denomination you were once part of, which left you wounded from poor leadership or teaching that distorted the gospel.

In my own life, as I reengaged with the Lord's Prayer in a much more deliberate way, I came to a point after months of praying this prayer daily where I was quite sure all faint flickers of unforgiveness had been rooted out of my heart. But then the Lord showed me the resentment in my heart against a former Prime Minister who had treated our region of Canada with particular distain. Even though he hadn't governed for decades, whenever his name came up, anger would rise in my heart. He had done grave damage to the moral fabric of the nation with laws he had brought in, so I had justified my resentment of him as "righteous anger". Because he was a political leader that I had no personal relationship with, resenting him somehow didn't seem to count in the same way. But the Lord showed me that regardless of what he had done, my resentment towards him was wrong. God knew that he had been an unrighteous leader, but in spite of that, I was called to love him and pray for him.

As well as forgiving people that we are not in relationship with but whose actions have affected us, we need to be willing to forgive in situations where things weren't done that should have been; sins of omission committed against us. That said, it's important to tread carefully here and not give room to criticism or attitudes of entitlement. None of us are the centre of the universe! However, there are legitimate places that others may have failed us. This could mean forgiving a parent who didn't affirm, forgiving church leadership for not giving us opportunities to serve or forgiving a friend who expects a relationship that is one-sided and tilted only towards their needs.

While I mentioned this in the last chapter, it bears repeating again: it's also time to forgive ourselves. This may be even more challenging than forgiving someone who has grievously wronged us but living in regret and self-condemnation is not the Father's heart for us. If God has forgiven us, we can't oppose him in this. We can't assert that our mistakes or sin are greater than his mercy.

Finally, we need to consider that we may harbour unvoiced anger and resentment towards God himself. Do we need to forgive God? While this sounds outrageous, for he can do no wrong, our hearts can interpret his dealings in our lives as harsh or unfaithful. We interpret what we think he has done, or not done, through a lens that judges his motives. This judgement will continually hinder our ability to trust him until we honestly acknowledge it, repent and ask for healing. If we are honest with the Father and ask him to speak to us about why it might be so hard to trust him, he will.

POWER OF FORGIVENESS

Becoming a vessel of the Father's forgiveness, one who forgives like the

Father forgives, is a privilege. It is a way of advancing his kingdom and increasing his glory. Even if no one knows that we have been sinned against, but we have still forgiven, the fragrance of Christ, his love and humility is released in a powerful way. Forgiveness is a spiritual climate changer. We can be sure that Stephen's forgiveness, given freely in the bloody moments during his murder, haunted Paul who had stood by observing and endorsing. This forgiveness was so clearly empowered by a supernatural love that Paul didn't have. The tangible presence and glory of God that permeated Stephen's forgiveness would have been like Paul having a direct encounter with the Lord, leaving him forever after unable to shake the impact of God's love on his heart.

NOT JUST FOR US

As we seek to follow Jesus more closely in his forgiveness, our lives open up to him and we find him cleansing our hearts much more deeply. From this place of having the log taken out of our eye, we become aware of how desperately this cleansing from unforgiveness is needed across the Church. Unforgiveness, resentment and bitterness have seeped into the Church at all levels and are ravaging our relationships and unity. These sins are pervasive and deep. Most Christians have at least some lingering, if not blatantly entrenched area of unforgiveness and we have become sleepily comfortable, accustomed to this status quo.

Unforgiveness has kept many relationships in a place of alienation, whether in marriages, families, businesses or between former friends. Entire groups within the Body of Christ have been alienated as churches or denominations have split, at times passing on offenses for the next generation to carry, mocking the other group in sermon illustrations or seminary classrooms.

These divisions lead to judgements, rivalry and all manner of broken, sinful reactions. Reactions where love and unity are absent. When we walk this way, we are actually fighting against the expressed desire of Jesus in his prayer of John 17—that we would be one.

UNTO UNITY

If the whole Church prayed even this small part of the Lord's Prayer daily and we genuinely meant it from our hearts, it would launch a stunning movement of repentance, reconciliation, restored love and unity throughout the Body of Christ. This would reverse the tide of division and as unity grew, the result would be an authority on our preaching, power in our prayers and the presence of God dwelling in our midst in a much more tangible, supernatural way. It would begin to look like revival.

The first step towards this wonderful kind of awakening is intercession. It's where all who see the need, who are stirred with Jesus' longing for his people to be one, who have personally asked him to keep their hearts free from all wisps of unforgiveness begin to pray. I believe the Holy Spirit is looking for intercessors like this in this hour, ones who in deep humility will war against unforgiveness whether found in their own hearts or in the ethos of the Church.

So, we pray, "...as we forgive", and as we do, we see that this could be the point of breakthrough into revival. This simple phrase, so packed with the radical love of God, could become the hinge of intercession that shifts everything. It could be the transforming prayer that empowers the Church to be the glorious, confounding, living illustration of God's love on earth.

The potential that this prayer carries makes it vital that we don't skip through it on a mere surface level, but allow it to transform our hearts and then open into intercession for the Church. As you pray, let faith grow for a move of God, mighty enough to dismantle fortified, even ancient divisions.

Another very important point of intercession is for those who are persecuting the Church. In these days, Christianity is the most persecuted faith in the world. This is most intense in Asia, the Middle East and Africa, but hostility towards Christianity is encroaching quickly into Western society. Persecution, even martyrdom of Christians is at the highest level ever in history, calling us to follow Jesus' instructions to bless those that curse us and pray for those who see themselves as our enemies.[107] The practice of serving those who hate us through genuine, loving intercession was very alive in the early Church, and undoubtedly a key factor in Paul coming to faith. When we in love, forgive and commit ourselves to pray, it connects our hearts with the Father's heart, filling us with his compassion. This posture of grace enables spiritual doors to open for the same kind of supernatural Damascus Road encounters that turned a zealous persecutor into an Apostle.

APPLYING IT IN PRAYER

Here are some approaches to this part of the prayer that may broaden the way you have previously prayed it.

- I forgive ____ for _____
- Let me forgive all who hurt me, as fully and deeply as you forgive
- Help me to love my neighbour as myself, by forgiving
- Shine your light into my heart and show me any hint of unforgiveness, even from past years
- Train my heart to forgive quickly; let this "spiritual muscle" be strong and ready to respond
- Grant supernatural grace for the places I am struggling to forgive; I lean on you
- May I not just forgive, but be healed from the impact of that sin against me
- Bring a revival of forgiveness into the Church
- Show us where we have held resentment against you Father, unravel this, forgive and heal us
- Heal marriages and families through forgiveness and reconciliation

---

107 Lu 6:28

- May all conflict in relationships be brought to peace before we take communion together
- Reconcile the generations, where parents and children have been estranged
- Grant pastors the boldness to uncompromisingly preach the requirement to forgive and the grace the Father makes available to help us do so
- Shift us away from expecting and condoning unforgiveness as the norm in the Church
- Have mercy on those that are violently persecuting Christians; meet them with your love
- Bring whole denominations and Church networks into reconciliation, don't let us continue in alienation and division

SCRIPTURES TO MEDITATE ON

- Jesus' example—Lk 23:34
- Stephen's example—Act 7:60
- Joseph's example—Gen 50:17-21
- Forgive so that the Father will forgive you—Mk 11:25,26
- Seventy-seven times—Mt 18:21-35
- Bear with each other—Col 3:13
- Freely—Mt 10:8
- Short accounts—Eph 4:26
- Return good for evil—1 Pt 3:9
- No bitterness—Eph 4:31
- No root of bitterness—Heb 12:15

GROUP DISCUSSION QUESTIONS:

1. Do you feel stuck in unforgiveness in some place in your life? Could the group pray for you in this?
2. What would it look like for quick, generous, forgiveness to be the norm in the Church? How would this lead us closer to revival?
3. Is extending forgiveness to yourself or to God something you have considered before?

Chapter Ten

LEAD US NOT

We now come to the part of the prayer where Jesus introduces us to the way of greater victory. After going deep into a place of repentance, cleansing and forgiving others, we are freshly aware of how easily we stumble. We are sensitized to how our hearts are hard-wired towards selfishness and how we so naturally deflect blame, justifying our ungodly motives. It's a sobering, humbling realization which thankfully shakes our confidence in the strength of our own righteousness. And at this point of weakness, Jesus is right here to give us his strength, to lead us into the way of gloriously overcoming.

We'll explore that way of victory, but before we go there, let's face the obvious issue that this petition presents. This is the issue that has caused many, unsure of how to pray it, to skip quickly over this petition and in doing so they have missed the power and grace it can release.

The petition of "Lead us not into temptation" has long been a source of difficulty for the Church as we hold it up against James' teaching that God does not tempt: *"Let no one say when he is tempted, "I am being tempted by God," for God cannot be tempted with evil, and he himself tempts no one. But each person is tempted when he is lured and enticed by his own desire. Then desire when it has conceived gives birth to sin, and sin when it is fully grown brings forth death."*[108]

This sense of conflict between asking the Father to lead us not into temptation and the truth that he never tempts requires that we look deeper to understand what's really going on in this petition. We need understanding to be able to fully benefit from praying it. There are two principles that will help us.

First, the concept that temptation and testing are two sides of the same coin. We are tested by God to strengthen us and give us opportunities to choose him. James again teaches us that this testing produces steadfastness and when steadfastness has its full effect, we will be complete and lacking nothing.[109] So testing is of great value. Testing refines and matures our faith.

But in the same situation, right at the point where we are being tested, an opportunity opens up for us to be tempted. It's as if in that situation, the Father is encouraging us to choose well and to choose victory over sin, but at the same time the enemy is actively preying on our weaknesses, enticing us to fall.

This leads us to our second principle, which is that we have an active and malicious tempter. The Devil is even given this name, "tempter" when he sought to tempt Jesus in the wilderness.[110] Jesus supremely overcame and so offers us his path of victory for every moment we are faced with temptation. So, this petition is a recognition of our dependence on his victory and a cry for that victory to consistently manifest in our daily places of temptation.

The early Church understood this concept and would often pray this petition in a paraphrased way, "let me not be led away into temptation". This remains a helpful way to pray as it reminds us that the "leading away" is not actively God, but the combination of our weaknesses and the active work of the enemy. We are asking that the Father would

108 Jas 1:13-15

109 Jas 1:4

110 Mt 4:3

lead us into Jesus' victory so that each place of testing would produce greater fruit of righteousness and union with him.

As we ask to not be led in one direction, we are in essence asking to be led in another direction: into the ways of Jesus. We are not standing still in neutral territory, we are still moving, but we desire to walk in Jesus' way and not in the way of sin. This petition is more than, "Help me not sin", it has a positive aspect as well and could trigger a prayer like, "May I be full of the fruit of the Spirit, may the very opposite of that which is now tempting me spring up!" For example, when you are tempted with anger, you would pray for patience and peace to abound. Remember Paul's words to us in Galatians, "But I say, walk by the Spirit, and you will not gratify the desires of the flesh."[111]

Walking by the Spirit involves a life that is filled with the fruit of the Spirit, but also a life that is patterned after Jesus in all of his ways. It's a life that consistently overcomes sin, the flesh, the world and stays in step with the rhythms and timing of the Holy Spirit. Imitating Jesus leads us into a healthier, holier lifestyle where we find temptations which previously so enticed us begin to fade in their appeal.

Consider for example, the following aspects of how Jesus walked. We can pray for these ways of living to be replicated in us as well. They all add to our understanding of the attitudes and values that strengthened Jesus' daily victory over temptation throughout his life. Considering these can inspire our prayers.

He walked as a son.

He knew who he was and was never out of communion with the Father. He was never disobedient or resistant to the Father's will. Jesus never stumbled into doubting the Father's love or affirmation, even for a moment. He walked perfectly before us as a Son so that we would know the Father and know how to live as children of God.

---

111 Gal 5:16

He walked as a servant.

He took on the most humble flesh and served all who sincerely came to him in need. He served in a wide variety of ways. For some it meant giving them truth, for others it was healing their blindness, while still others on the fringes of society were served with the time he took to join them for a meal.

He walked as a teacher.

All that he did revealed the Father and discipled those that would follow. He taught with words and deeds, with his attitude, with what he was zealous for, in his work ethic, his faith, and his unwillingness to shrink back from the cross.

He walked in rest.

Jesus lived in a deep peaceful shalom, void of anxiety or strife. He wouldn't be pressured into doing anything beyond what the Father was doing, even though at times, doing the Father's will, meant his days were long and demanding.[112]

He walked in power.

Jesus demonstrated power over all sickness, death, demonic powers and even over the wind and storms. His words, presence, prayers and touch were all filled with supernatural power. He rose from death in power, with a glorified and eternally resurrected body, utterly defeating death and the fear with which it enslaved mankind.

He walked in trust.

Jesus trusted the Father in all ways and in the most extreme situations.

112 Jn 5:19

He received upon himself the full torrent of the Father's wrath for all mankind's sin on the cross and then, still, with his last words, entrusted his spirit to the Father to resurrect him.[113]

He walked on mission.

Jesus was sent by the Father with a mission to seek and save, to reveal the Father and to destroy the works of the enemy.[114] He stayed in this posture of the "sent one" throughout his life, living with purpose, a clear vision and calling. Nothing would distract him from his mission.

So, this is not a "fly-over" petition. It gives us space to thoroughly pray that our lives would overcome the way Jesus did.

WATCH AND PRAY

Even though there is much to be gained from praying this petition, it is very likely the most under-prayed portion of the entire prayer. We seem disconnected from the need to pray it. Jesus emphasizes it again in the hours before the cross. He calls his disciples to *"Watch and pray, that you may not enter into temptation. The spirit is indeed willing, but the flesh is weak."*[115] In this exhortation he's reemphasizing how important this petition is and expanding it by adding to it the practice of watching. He knew we needed to be alert and mindful of how we were being tempted so that we would lean on him for power to resist.

Let's give some thought to the ways that we are drawn into temptation which could be avoided if we would remain vigilant and watchful, rather than just sleepily stumbling along as we are prone to do. One of the factors that is not always considered would be what we might call the spiritual environment or climate. A spiritual climate can be markedly influenced by others in the family or church community;

113 Lk 23:46
114 Lk 19:10, Jn 17:25-26, 1Jn 3:8
115 Mk 14:38

are they striving, fearful, grumbling? These sins and others like them can easily spread if we are not alert. Thankfully, virtues like holiness, honour and love can also spread as we provoke one another to good deeds. The corporate level of the fruit and the life of the Spirit is the main determining factor in our spiritual climate. But when a Christian community condones a sin so that it becomes widespread, the spiritual climate of that community deteriorates. This creates a momentum and a pull towards that particular sin, making it harder to resist. In these situations, we need to notice and proactively choose to walk a different way. "Lead us not into temptation".

Sin opens a door to demonic influences and so another important factor when we consider our spiritual climate is to recognize how the enemy may be involved. He may actively be working to promote sin and bring destruction with his presence in the spiritual climate. He may also be targeting individuals directly. The devil is a vicious, always-playing-dirty enemy poised to jump in and make matters worse, taking advantage of our weakest areas and kicking us while we are down. Watching and praying involves being aware of when he is ramping up his influence. It's staying clothed in our spiritual armour. We'll unpack this more extensively in the next chapter, as we focus on "Deliver us from evil".

The spirit of the world also poses a real place of temptation for us, so watching includes identifying its influence. Many times, we will actually adopt the values or ways of the world, while cloaking them in Christian language or using them for Christian purposes. Being aware of how easily we can fall into this is an important part of watching.

But the most challenging source of temptation is not external; it's from our own heart. This is what we read earlier in James 1: "we are enticed by our own desires." Although this is where we need to be most vigilantly watching and praying, in our Western Christian culture the topic of sin is frequently avoided in favour of more palatable topics by those who equip the Church. This lack of teaching renders us dull and blithely unaware of sin's pernicious reality. We've lost much self-awareness of our weakness and become oblivious to temptations that are all around us. If and when we do notice temptation, we've slipped into an overly optimistic confidence in our ability to resist it.

If we don't agree with our Father's assessment of how horrible sin is, (and thus share in His perfect hatred of it), we don't mind falling into a bit of sin here and there. But Jesus wants to lead us in a different way, a way where we become fiercely drawn to the beauty of holiness and long to be like the Holy One. For this, we need to watch and pray.

COME INTO THE LIGHT

If we pause and consider some of the most common temptations that Christians face, we can suddenly see with even greater clarity why we need this prayer. These could be temptations that if acted on become sin, or even temptations to wallow in negative emotions that could lead us into sin. Their reality in all of our lives makes praying this prayer vital.

In times of revival, there has almost universally been a renewed revelation of God's holiness which brings a stark awareness of sin, like a bright light suddenly shining. In that light, all that has been happily hiding and multiplying in the darkness is now seen. The altars of repentance fill with seemingly upright, model Christians now appalled at how backslidden their hearts had become. In the Lord's Prayer, a prayer that's all about revival, Jesus leads us from a cry for cleansing (forgive us our sins) to pressing in for transformation and victory in the very place where we've stumbled. It's not his heart for us to only be cleansed, then to repeatedly fall in the same way. He has come to set us free. He is able to take us from this place of chronic stumbling to a testimony of his strength perfected in our weakness.

Because of our spiritual dullness outside of these seasons of revival, it's helpful to consider some of the temptations that are common to all of us in any culture or generation. There may be a few that you recognize as trouble spots in your own life, so this list could help you to proactively pray that you would walk in a different, Spirit-empowered way. This list could also provoke you to intercede for your congregation, denomination or the Body of Christ to marvellously overcome in these areas of struggle. It is not meant to be a comprehensive list, but rather a help towards self-awareness. The Holy Spirit always has your redemption and victory as his goal, so ask him to speak to you as you ponder these various areas of temptation. Listen to his voice and at the same time refuse to give ear to the enemy's voice of accusation and hopelessness.

COMMON AREAS OF TEMPTATION

- Pride – which could also include ego, narcissism, vanity and false humility. Consider how much time and thought goes into your image in the eyes of others. False humility is the flip side of this coin, where we adopt a self-image of unworthiness, weakness, or inferiority, refusing to yield this self-image to the transformation of the Spirit.
- Self-righteousness – this is probably much more pervasive and subtle than we think. It takes enjoyment in reflecting on one's spiritual achievements, subtly (or not so) presuming these achievements grant an increased standing with God. It's illustrated in the parable of the sinner and the pharisee.[116]
- Independence – trying to be like God, without dependence on God. This is the root of self-sufficiency, self-promotion, striving and man's works. When we walk independently from God, we trust ourselves rather than him. It is also a root cause for isolating from others in the body of Christ.
- Unbelief – while faith is something we all seek to grow in, there are times when we resist believing. We don't respond to what God has said, what He's promised or the truth about His character. Consider Hebrews 3:12.
- Division – we all have a natural propensity towards esteeming our group, race, nationality, political leaning, generation or

116 Lk 18:10-14

denomination above others. This perspective has no place in the kingdom reality of oneness in Christ. It is this elitist attitude that is addressed by the exhortation to not think more highly of ourselves than we ought.[117]

- Lukewarmness – spiritual apathy and lack of love, interest or pursuit of God. Because there is no investment in spiritual disciplines to pursue God, we end up drifting further from him, carried by the current of the spirit of the world.
- Fear – while fear itself is not a sin, being *controlled* by the fear of man or other fears can be. These fears can hold us back from wholehearted obedience or being a bold witness. In the New Testament there is a frequent call to courage, even in the face of great opposition.
- Anxiety and Worry – this is everywhere, but God can lead us out of it, into trust and peace. His solution for anxiety is that we give him our cares in the place of prayer as we choose to believe the truth of his goodness.[118]
- Worldliness – this is an alignment of our mindset, value system or lifestyle with that of the surrounding secular culture. We often try to be friends with the world, but scripture tells us this puts us at enmity with God.[119] Worldliness entices us to agree with its accusations against God while still trying to walk with him. We try to live a watered-down Christian life, so we are not subjected to the scorn and rejection that Jesus is treated with.
- Lust and Immorality – this encompasses a wide range of weaknesses and sins which are an issue for both men and women. With our sex-saturated culture, sexual purity, in actions, words and thoughts is an area that must be guarded diligently

117 Rom 12:3
118 1 Pt 5:7, Phil 4:6-7
119 Jas 4:4

and proactively. The answer is not to just lower our standards.

- Love of Money – scriptures reveal that this is the root of all kinds of evil, so it's vital that we watch over our hearts that they wouldn't be seduced by money's enticements.[120] One of the fruits of the love of money is greed. Hoarding, grasping, financial opportunism and withholding are all types of greed.
- Selfishness – this also involves inordinate self-love. It's putting ourselves first, seeking to be served rather than serving, using people for our gain. It's the antithesis of genuine agape love (God's love) where the motivation is 'your good at my expense'.
- Judgement – we can be quick to assess someone's motives or intentions in a negative light and fall into judgment. We may not have any awareness of the struggles and difficulties others have battled through, nor see the whole picture and all the factors. It's easy to hold others to a standard we don't hold ourselves to. Even while we judge, we often expect others to discern our intentions with grace and mercy.
- Unforgiveness – this can easily lead to resentment, bitterness, a desire for vengeance and malice. We wish those who have hurt us or sinned against us harm, relishing it when they suffer.
- Disobedience – being unresponsive to the Spirit, not listening, not honouring the scriptures, not obeying what God has clearly shown you to do either through the Bible or by the Spirit.
- Idolatry – allowing any created thing to become the centre of your attention, affections, worship or dependence. Any way that you look to created things to provide what you need rather than God is a form of idolatry. This is much bigger than the worship of idolatrous carvings, like we see in the Old Testament. This is perhaps the most heinous of all sins.

---

120 1 Tim 6:10

- Thanklessness – when we lack gratitude for all that God has done and the immenseness of his grace towards us, our hearts slowly become darkened and hardened. Thanklessness towards God grows into thanklessness towards others. We begin to take those around us for granted, assuming we are entitled to receive blessings and kindness from them. Thanklessness leads to murmuring and complaining.
- Lust for Power – this can manifest in overt ways of seeking fame, money or position because of the power these may grant. It can also show up in much more subtle ways where we manipulate or seek to control others in our hunger for power.
- Hardheartedness – similar to lukewarmness but involves indifference and lack of compassion toward our fellow man. We are not moved to act, pray, serve or give by the same compassion that moves Jesus. This can also be toward the Lord, where a hard heart means being cold and unmoved instead of responding with thanksgiving, repentance, worship or awe.
- Laziness – while not often spoken about, laziness is indeed a sin and will lead us into the love of comfort, ease and convenience, avoiding all kinds of sacrifice. It will perpetually direct us to take the easy way rather than that which will most glorify God. It's an indulgence of the flesh.
- Hypocrisy – when we are tempted to present an image of ourselves better than reality, we are being tempted by hypocrisy, rooted in pride. Hypocrisy is where we would advocate for virtue, without cultivating it in our lives. It's the talk without the walk.
- Avoiding the Cross – this can either be being ashamed of the gospel or an attempt to preserve our "self-life", by skirting the cross, avoiding its confrontation of our hearts. This can mean pursuing outward change through motivational self-help, good works or even a social gospel.

- Lack of Care for the Poor – a mindset that doesn't build care for the poor into our lifestyle. This includes caring for the broken, the ill, the rejected, the orphaned, oppressed and impoverished.
- Envy – the sinful emotion of displeasure with another's success, possessions or favour. It's often the root of ungodly comparisons and competition. A sister emotion is jealousy, the anxiety that someone else will take what we have, an anxiety that can lead to all kinds of ungodly reactions as we try to control and protect what we feel is ours. Both of these are intensely powerful emotions. Remember, the first murder was the fruit of jealousy.

While this might seem like a rather long and depressing list of sins, defining them actually equips us to be more watchful, more spiritually aware and sensitive. Being watchful and asking the Father to "Lead us not into temptation" is a posture of humility and dependence on the Spirit. It is not becoming hyper-focused on sin, nor living in anxiety that we might stumble.

Finally, before we leave this topic of temptation it's important to reinforce the truth that being tempted is vastly different than sinning. There is no shame in being tempted. Jesus himself was tempted but did not sin. *"For we do not have a high priest who is unable to sympathize with our weaknesses, but one who in every respect has been tempted as we are, yet without sin."*[121]

We will be tempted all the days of our lives. We don't outgrow temptation or mature into needing Jesus less. But each of these points of weakness where we could potentially fall gives us an opportunity to cling to the Great High Priest in communion and prayer. He has promised to provide us all the grace and mercy we need for our weakness; a provision that is sufficient and abundant.[122]

---

121 Heb 4:15
122 Heb 4:16

APPLYING IT IN PRAYER

As we have done with the previous petitions, let's consider some of the different applications and the ways "Lead us not into temptation" could be prayed.

- Don't let me to be led away into temptation, keep my feet on the path toward you
- You know my weakness towards ________, strengthen me to walk without stumbling in this again
- Help me to watch and pray, staying spiritually alert and in communion with you
- Lead me in boldness in __________ situation where I naturally default to fear
- Sharpen my discernment to what is negatively influencing my walk
- Lead me away from any demonic snares or entrapments
- Grant me deeper revelation of how Jesus walked as a Son, so that I could imitate him.
- Lead our church in Jesus' way of walking; in trust, rest and great fruitfulness—not striving
- Lead us away from the fear of man
- Build humility into my life that I would be continually aware of my dependence on you
- Show me where I am going my own way in self-reliant independence
- Uproot the love of money from my heart, may it not colour my priorities or decisions
- Empower me to live a life where my goal is to serve, not be served

- Allow a love for holiness to grow in my heart

SCRIPTURES TO MEDITIATE ON

- Rise and pray—Lk 22:46
- Common to man—1 Cor 10:13
- The Lord preserves—Ps 121:7
- Watch and pray—Mt 26:41
- Not taken out of the world—Jn 17:15
- Temptation of money—1 Tim 6:9
- Pure devotion to Christ—2 Cor 11:3
- He will establish us and keep us—2 Thes 3:3
- Lead me in the everlasting way—Ps 139:24
- Lead me in righteousness—Ps 5:8
- Walk in the Spirit—Gal 5:16
- Pursue purity—2 Cor 7:1
- Lust of the flesh—1 Jn 2:16
- He will wholly sanctify us—1 Thes 5:23

GROUP DISCUSSION QUESTIONS:

1. Describe the difference between depending on Jesus when facing temptation and resisting temptation in our own strength.
2. How can we cultivate healthy watchfulness in our lives and church communities?
3. Talk about the statement that this petition is the least prayed part of the Lord's Prayer. Why do you think this is?
4. What is your heart's response to "There is no shame in being tempted."?

Chapter Eleven

DELIVER US

In our journey through the Lord's Prayer, we have arrived at the final petition, which is placed last intentionally but should never be omitted. This petition has traditionally been translated from the original Greek as "But deliver us from evil" but an equally correct translation is "But deliver us from the evil one." The breadth of meaning we find in the Greek give us instruction and faith to pray for deliverance from every type and source of evil. However, it gives particular emphasis to deliverance from the devil. Here we ask to be delivered from all the demonic schemes employed to destroy our lives, families and churches as well as the schemes the enemy uses to harden hearts of unbelievers against God.

It's fitting that Jesus addresses the demonic in the very last petition. This teaches us much about his attitude and perspective towards the devil and his work. Jesus doesn't deny that the devil is real or is intent on harming the people of God and opposing the Father in any way that he can, but he also doesn't focus on him. In fact, he deals with Satan last.

Over the last few decades, an approach to prayer called spiritual warfare has emerged and developed, with much understanding about how the enemy works. Some of this has been biblical, but some has been conjecture, which has led away from a biblical perspective. The biblical understanding of spiritual warfare (for example, the enemy lies, sows doubt and accuses) gives us greater discernment and wisdom in prayer. But the unbiblical understanding is inordinately focused on the enemy as the source of all our struggles and ascribes to him the ability to attack us at every turn. In this paradigm, so much time is spent discerning how the enemy is involved and opposing him in prayer, that we fall into believing he has much more power, influence and access to our lives than he actually does. Ironically, this undue focus creates a fearful lifestyle that actually *does* give him access—through our fear.

As is human nature, when this spiritual warfare approach grew, it triggered a reaction to its imbalance and fear. It's like the pendulum that swings too far one way, provoking us to react, but then swings too far in the opposite direction. Thus many, in reaction to the excesses of the spiritual warfare teaching now virtually deny the enemy's influence at all. This swing of the pendulum is no more biblical or healthy than the excessive spiritual warfare approach, for it allows the enemy unchecked freedom to attack individuals, families or churches. No one resists him, no one rebukes him. Thankfully Jesus offers us wisdom, perspective and success in dealing with the demonic. He is neither fearfully obsessed nor in denial that the devil is actively opposing him. He is the ultimate Overcomer and delighted to train us in this.

While this petition encompasses a deliverance from evil beyond just the demonic, let's begin here, by looking briefly at the varying levels of demonic influence that could impact the life of a believer. If this is an issue for you, the level of influence the enemy has will determine how you pray for deliverance. Your approach will depend on the prevalence and level of access that this demonic spirit has had in your life or your family.

Major demonic influence

At this level, there is extreme and intense influence from the demonic.

Deliverance comes through exorcising the demonic spirit, (or spirits) that have attached to your soul. Spirits that are demonic will torment you with their continual presence, pressure you to sin and cloud your revelation of Jesus. Jesus has made full provision for your deliverance from all spirits; they have no power to resist him. He came to set the captives free and he's singularly good at it.

If you feel this might be your situation, the best course of action is to seek out a pastor who can pray you through the steps needed to be fully delivered and set free. The worst course of action is to do nothing, to be ashamed or determine you'll just overcome on your own by the strength of your will.

Demonic access

To delve into the ways that the enemy can have access to a Christian's life is beyond the scope of this book but giving a simple overview may still prove helpful.[123] Essentially, demonic access is where the enemy, through our neglect or sin, has found a way to influence us. The best way to think of this concept may be to consider that we have opened a door (through sin) or neglected to close a door (that others, or our situation has opened). The level of influence from this open door can range from subtle to dramatic, from a private struggle to a full-blown ravaging of our families or churches, all from a door of access left open. Regardless of the scope or level of intensity, putting a stop to the destruction involves identifying the door that is open, repenting (if necessary) and closing the door. Once this is done, we renounce and rebuke the access the enemy has had.

Jesus demonstrates his great wisdom by placing this petition of "Deliver us from evil" last in the Lord's Prayer. By the time we get here, he has already led us through all the other petitions, each one potentially

---

123 These books are recommended as a further resource for understanding deliverance:
James Goll, *Deliverance From Darkness: The Essential Guide to Defeating Demonic Strongholds and Oppression* (Grand Rapids, MI: Chosen Books, 2010).
Derek Prince, *They Shall Expel Demons* (Grand Rapids, MI: Chosen Books, 1998).

closing doors of access that the enemy could have had in our lives. As we've prayed through the Prayer, we've taken time to deeply yield our will, we've repented of all known sin, we've forgiven all who might have sinned against us and now we are ready to ask to be delivered. We simply look to the Father and ask him, in full faith, to "Deliver us from the evil one!"

We don't have to cry and plead; he has instructed us to pray this, so we can be completely confident that he will answer. When we turn with heart-felt repentance and ask for his forgiveness, we have great confidence that he will answer and forgive. We can apply this same confident faith to the request for deliverance and freedom. The average individual who has identified, repented and closed the door of access that the enemy was using will find a quick answer to their prayer for deliverance. There are some individuals with more severe situations, where the enemy has held deeply established access to our lives and these require additional steps and support. In these situations, we don't fight alone. We turn to our Christian community and walk towards freedom with the added strength that the support of other believers affords. A season of fasting and prayer may also be needed to firmly close those spiritual doors and keep them closed. But even in these more severe settings, deliverance is promised.

> *"I [Jesus] will no longer talk much with you, for the ruler of this world is coming. He has no claim on me." Jn 14:30.*

Spiritual attack

All Christians experience the buffeting of demonic, spiritual attack from time to time. These are typically launched against us in the moments when we or our churches are the most vulnerable. Jesus experienced this, as did all the Apostles, so don't be surprised or fearful. Attacks are strategically planned by the enemy to harm, hinder or abort the Father's plans and purposes, yet the Father uses them to teach us to overcome in Christ. Spiritual attacks are just for a time, differing from the continual access that comes from an open door, but like open door access, there is a wide range to their intensity. They can be mild and barely discernible or come in a cluster, buffeting and disorienting us with major body blows. They manifest the enemy's malicious intent to steal, kill and destroy.[124]

When these attacks flare up, praying "Deliver us from the evil one" with faith and fervency will disarm them, rendering them greatly reduced or completely arrested. Thankfully we are not always in a time of spiritual attack; our norm is an abundant life rich with peace, blessing and joy. How then, in these times of peace should we pray this petition?

If we and the others we pray for don't have a need for deliverance from attack, then we pray this petition as a preemptive prayer for divine protection against all demonic activity, so that it would be cut off before it even appears. This is how Jesus prayed for us in the Garden of Gethsemane.[125]

The influence of excessive teaching on spiritual warfare has created a sense of anxiety in many hearts, that rises whenever the demonic needs to be addressed. This tempts us to skirt this prayer. For others, it has created alarm that we must pray everything exactly right, as if our prayer was a magic spell that would backfire if not properly spoken. There is no need for fear. We are praying to our loving Father and our faith is in our Father, not our perfect prayer.

We pray in faith for protection and deliverance from every attack that the enemy has set against us, be it physical, financial, emotional, mental, relational or spiritual. Praying this regularly, under the leading of the Spirit, dramatically increases divine protection and brings peace into our lives. We look to the Father for his good gifts, including his protection, rather than continually bracing for "backlash" or attack. We do not fear the enemy and his threats to punish us for kingdom advances.

"But he gives more grace. Therefore it says, "God opposes the proud, but gives grace to the humble." Submit yourselves therefore to God. Resist the devil, and he will flee from you." Jas 4:6-7

---

124 Jn10:10
125 Jn 17:15

SEASONS OF SUFFERING

While it's a biblical practice to ask for God's protection, we shouldn't paint a picture that we can always expect blissful, comfortable lives and anything less than that ideal is the result of spiritual attack. There will be times for all of us when the protection of the Father partially lifts. These are times where the enemy is allowed by the Father to test us, refine us and strip away things that are distracting us. The Father's purpose is to deepen our dependence and communion with him, which can only happen through weakness.

The Old Testament contains many examples of God's testing which involves suffering, such as in the lives of Job, David, Hannah, Joseph and others. But testing through suffering is also for the New Testament age and was the experience of Jesus and the early Church.[126] Yet even in the midst of the fiercest flames, we remain in the Father's hand and he is absolutely in control. He is completely capable of retooling any form of suffering that the enemy brings into an instrument that works together for our ultimate good. He hasn't abandoned us or stopped being our protector for even a heartbeat.

Our response to suffering can be either clinging to the Lord in humility and raw trust or leaving his side in anger and bitterness. We have this choice. If we choose to cling, even while we don't understand, we gain precious treasures: the fellowship of his sufferings, a tenderized heart and much more grace for others. Consider Job's famous declaration while in the midst of the confusion of suffering at the enemy's hand: *"Though he [God] slay me yet will I trust him."* (Job 13:15a NKJV).

In these seasons of suffering, stress or persecution, we ask the Father to lead us through quickly and deliver us, while still staying submitted to his timing and not demanding our own.

---

126 Mt 4:1-11, Lk 22:31-32, 1 Pt 4:12-13

FATHER OF LIES

As we earnestly pray the petition of "Deliver us from the evil one", there are three additional areas (besides tempting) that we should become more attentive to, as they flow out of the devil's intrinsic nature. Jesus called him the "father of lies" and in the book of Revelation he is called the "accuser of the brethren" and the "deceiver of the whole world".[127] With this in mind, we need to be aware that along with tempting, the enemy also attacks by lying, accusing and deceiving.

While the devil rages against the Church with uncontrolled anger, his most intense hatred is towards God himself. The enemy continually lies to us about God, his nature, his motives and his trustworthiness. He does all that he can to distort our revelation of the Lord and our understanding of his ways, using accusations and deception. This was the nature of the very first interaction he had with man in the garden, as he subtly accused God of withholding blessings from Adam and Eve, out of selfish motives. In the devil's desire to hurt God, he makes every attempt to hurt us, cause us to sin and alienate us from the Father. As we pray, "Deliver us from the evil one," ask the Father to reveal any deceptions you have stumbled into and any lies you have believed about God. The heart of the enemy's evil is his continual, slandering lies about God.

While God himself is the focal point of the most intense demonic efforts of lying, accusing and deceiving, the enemy doesn't stop there. He will also seek to lie to you about who God has made you to be, your worth and your standing in Christ. He will accuse and condemn you if you make room for his voice. The enemy will also craft accusations against your Christian brothers and sisters so that you become suspicious of their motives and your relationships deteriorate. Don't be enticed into agreeing with his accusations against God, yourself or others in your heart. Deliver us from the evil one.

Deception was a great concern in the early Church and the Apostles

---

127 Jn 8:44, Rev 12:10, Rev 12:9

fought to protect the gospel from all manner of distortions, even outright heresy. The enemy has not stopped using this tactic, even though we are generally much less alert to it. We live in a time where most Christians in the Western Church self-feed. We look to podcasts, books and video teachings on YouTube by well-known preachers to supplement our Sunday morning experience, trusting implicitly what is being taught because of the power of their celebrity. This creates a perfect opportunity for a subtle or even blatant distortion of the gospel towards one that is more man-centred, works-oriented or fleshly; a path towards deception. Don't forget, deception would never be successful if it wasn't appealing! As we regularly pray to be delivered from evil, even if we have inadvertently been deceived, the Father will deliver us. He will gently reveal the lies, sharpen our discernment and lead us into the truth.

All of this intercession for deliverance from the activity of the enemy should be prayed personally for our lives but also for our churches and communities. Reflect for a moment on how much the enemy hates revival; how much he hates people coming to Christ in widespread moves of God and how much he hates the Church returning to passion for Jesus. What he hates he will oppose. Spirit-led intercession can sabotage his evil intentions, while simultaneously releasing the Father's protection over the tender shoots of revival.

DIFFERENT KINDS OF EVIL

We've looked at some of the ways this petition can be applied to be a prayer of deliverance from the evil one, the devil, but this petition is also accurately expressed as, "Deliver us from evil" which includes all the other forms of evil that ravage our world. This is oppression and wickedness; the intentional, cruel, and malicious evil we see in the world around us.

Praying to be delivered from evil in this context is intercession for righteousness, justice and truth to increase, bringing light into the darkness. We intercede for the Lord to raise up righteous leaders, bosses, judges, university professors or governmental leaders who would choose God's ways. We further pray for righteous laws and policies to be adopted in our society; laws which value God's heart for the poor, for families, for the environment and more.

But evil is also the marring effects of sin, the brokenness of relationships, disease, natural disasters and poverty. The fall of man in the Garden has set in motion catastrophic brokenness in our once perfect world. The continual rejection of God adds to the weight of sin the world bears, so that all creation groans for the return of Christ, who will set all wrong things right. With this in mind, we intercede for the intervention of that which is good, which heals, serves, renews and rebuilds, counteracting the impact of evil.

We also contend in prayer for the oppressed. The most frequent victims of injustice and those who bear the greatest suffering at the hands of wickedness in our society are the weak—those without a voice to give them power. But the Father hears the cry of the widow and the fatherless, the poor and the struggling and he charges his Church to be his hands and voice on their behalf. He charges us to be a voice of justice. This must be done in practical and meaningful ways in addition to prayer. May we be authentically moved by the compassion of Jesus as we pray and at the same time, active in serving the needs.

STANDING TOGETHER

We are praying to Our Father who sees all the needs and brokenness around us. And the prayer Jesus has given us is oriented towards community rather than individualism, (observe that everything is framed as "us" and "our"), so when we ask to be delivered from evil, this too is corporate. Our hearts are drawn to intercede for those brothers and sisters that are facing persecution, imprisonment, torture or martyrdom for their faith. We also pray for those who are impoverished, disabled or struggling with illness. We may not know their names or faces, but we are exhorted to stand with them in prayer. This is what a true family does; we don't forget the ones that are suffering.

The evil we ask to be delivered from can be demonic activity and influence or it may be the everyday evil of our troubled society, but there is also a third major application. It can also be evil within us: the unredeemed, self-centred words, deeds or attitudes that wound others. At times our past emotional wounds cause us to overreact and wound others. Father, deliver us from this.

Let's also pray that the Father will deliver us from unconsciously being the source of evil. Well-meaning, but poorly conceived mission trips, foolish interactions with addicts and insensitively worded testimonies are examples of that which was intended as a blessing becoming something hurtful. We can be oblivious of how we impact those around us, even turning them away from Christ, simply out of foolishness. Therefore this petition is a powerful prayer that the Father would restrain us from being anything other than a vessel of blessing.

As we pray in this way, asking to bring the love and light of Jesus into every situation and relationship, the Father will hear our prayer and increase our holiness, sensitivity and wisdom. He'll mature us to care more skillfully for those around us.

DELIVERERS

After considering the many ways the Father delivers us and establishes us in security, away from evil's reach, our hearts should fill with praise! But he doesn't just deliver us and secure us, he empowers us to be like him, to be deliverers. He doesn't leave us helplessly watching the grinding, heart-wrenching destruction of evil in the world. He calls us to be co-labourers, co-deliverers, bringing his freedom and justice. This might be one life at a time or it might be strategically reforming evil systems that affect the lives of millions. Whatever our role, we should celebrate the victory he has secured for us and the empowerment he gives us to bring deliverance.

APPLYING IT IN PRAYER

Here are some ways this petition could be applied in prayer:

- Deliver me from (specific spirit)'s influence in my life
- Show me any open door where a demonic spirit has access to my life or family
- Cleanse me and wash me from the defilement the enemy has brought upon my life
- May I be brought into complete freedom, that you would be the only spiritual influence in my life
- Thank you for your great power to deliver me and my family
- May corporate deliverance spontaneously erupt in the midst of our worship services, let chains break!
- Deliver me from any distortion of the gospel that I have accepted; renew my mind.
- Show me any lies that I have believed about you, or about myself—deliver me from these
- Teach me to discern when I am facing spiritual attack and not just having a bad day; teach me to resist the devil rather than being his victim
- Forgive me for agreeing with the accuser of the brethren and holding accusation in my heart towards another Christian, rather than praying for them
- Grant me your perspective on the demonic so that I would join in your victory
- In this season of suffering, grant me the grace to trust you all the more
- Deliver our brothers and sisters who are facing persecution and oppression
- Make me like you—let me bring your deliverance to others in my community
- Establish justice for those living in systemic poverty

- Grant our government a heart of true righteousness and justice
- Fill our church with wisdom so that we would be used effectively to bring your deliverance as we go on mission
- Restrain me from being an unwitting source of evil

SCRIPTURES TO MEDITATE ON

- Destroy the work of the devil—1 Jn 3:8
- Set captives free—Lk 4:18
- After you have suffered—1 Pt 5:10
- Resist the devil—Jas 4:7
- Evil generation—Phil 2:15
- The Lord our Deliverer—Ps18:2
- Great Commission—Mk 16:17
- Esther—Est 4:14
- Joseph—Gen 50:20
- Father of Lies—Jn 8:44
- Wrestle not—Eph 6:12
- Deliver from wicked and evil men—2 Thes 3:1-3

GROUP DISCUSSION QUESTIONS:

1. Consider the two extremes when thinking about the devil: a) becoming fearful of his power and b) ignoring the reality of his warfare against us. Which extreme is more tempting for you?
2. How does the idea that the devil's greatest lies are about God make you feel?
3. Community plays a very important role in us being delivered from evil. Why?

Chapter Twelve

FOR EVER AND EVER

The concluding doxology of the Lord's Prayer, "For yours is the kingdom, the power and the glory, for ever and ever, amen" is not in the original text of Jesus' words but was added in the first centuries by the Church Fathers. It is a fitting explosion of worship, victory and praise to close our journey through each of the prayer's petitions. It is not a superfluous add-on; it actually serves as a truly important part of the prayer. It seals, it guides us to respond in praise and it refocuses us beautifully. We are being discipled by Jesus through the ones that he discipled, so following the Church Father's lead in this is great wisdom.

Throughout the Prayer, we have been asking for all that is in heaven to come to earth. The heavenly pattern that we see in the book of Revelation is that when God acts (or the angels worship) the Church (represented by the twenty-four elders) responds. The elders fall down in worship, casting down their crowns before the Lamb and crying "Amen!"

This doxology can be viewed as a response of worship similar to the worship of the elders. Our worship is triggered by the glorious activity of God which was set in motion by the prayer being prayed. We prayed, God moved in response and now we worship. It's the pattern of heaven coming to earth. It is worship that is full of faith, confident that the Father has heard us and responded, to the point that many of the answers to these prayers have already been granted. The worship of the doxology is like us casting down "our crowns" and it is entirely the right response. Declaring "amen" is our robust agreement, mirroring the "amen" in heaven. The Church Fathers have taught us well.

The words the Church Fathers chose are triune in nature, reflecting the trinity of God and the trinity of the three opening petitions, but they are essentially a simplified version of David's worship on the occasion of Solomon's coronation.[128] It's a fitting choice: in essence we are crowning the Son who is the King—Jesus, with our praise.

THE PERFECT PROGRESSION

When you look at the text of the Lord's Prayer, found in Luke 11 and Matthew 6, you notice that while these accounts differ slightly in petitions, the order of these petitions is absolutely consistent. The sequence is purposeful, beginning with "Our Father", or "Father", and moving through various petitions to either "Deliver us from evil", or "Lead us not into temptation".

The sequence speaks to us of the priority of loving God as the first and greatest commandment. It gives us a way to love him through our prayer as we pursue the reverence of his name, the increase of his kingdom and his will being done. Then the prayer leads us in this journey to pray for where the substance of heaven is needed on earth, a cry to give us this day either spiritual or natural bread. From this point the prayer guides us into a longing for holiness, a longing to be like Jesus, so we seek cleansing from all known sin. We receive his washing and refreshing and then, with deeply grateful hearts, overwhelmed with his love, we extend that love to others in forgiveness. What a beautiful progression! The prayer continues, and from this place of a clean, forgiving heart, we pray that we will be led towards him and away from all which so easily trips us up, including the enemy's evil plans.

---

128 1 Chron 29:11

We have just walked an incredible journey: stepping through the gate of glory with the opening of "Our Father", with each petition preparing us for the next, each one taking us deeper into his victory and blessing. Finally, we seal the prayer with exuberant praise.

In the previous petition, we have been addressing evil in all its forms. If the prayer ended there, it would leave our hearts focused on the works of darkness. If we were to stop here, allowing our minds to linger on thoughts of how the enemy might be working and the tragic ways people have been ravaged by him, we can settle into sorrow and possibly even fear or unbelief. It is much better that we refocus on Jesus and the greatness of his plan, his kingdom and his victory. While praying for deliverance from evil and addressing the works of darkness is necessary, it can be toxic to retain darkness as your focus. Every homeowner takes out the garbage but doesn't linger beside the garbage cans! Instead, they dispose of the garbage, secure the lid on the can and go back inside, even washing their hands to ensure there is no residual bacteria.

In the same way, at this point of the prayer our full attention and worship is lifted to the Father. "For yours is…" could be paraphrased as "because yours is". It's a recognition that we are praying all these things because of the greatness, majesty and unshakable, eternal power of the Father. The granting of all these requests is possible, even expected because "yours is…"

The doxology is glorious worship because we have just given ourselves to pray in the most effective way possible, which will result in the advance of the kingdom of God. We have just journeyed through the prayer that Jesus gave us, aligning with him, praying in his name. He is the Righteous Man, so these prayers are powerful and effective.[129] How could we hold back praise to the One who has heard our cries and is now moving on our behalf!

---

129 Jas 5:16

NO SECOND GUESSING

At times in prayer, we can feel as though we've been carried along with the momentum and have stepped out, praying a bold prayer that suddenly seems too big. Have we asked too much? Is it too impossible? We are tempted in that moment to scale back our request to something "more reasonable", to walk it back from the bold audacity we have just stepped into. Perhaps we back away from what we've just prayed by correcting ourselves, asking for something that is a more modest, incremental blessing, rather than a supernatural breakthrough.

If we've simply ventured into a bit of grandiose imagination, this walking back is appropriate, but if we were actually led by the Spirit to ask boldly, to ask grandly, we must fight to stand in faith. It helps us to know that one of unbelief's most predictable points of attack will be on the heels of bold prayer.

One of the great blessings of the doxology is that it shuts down that attack of unbelief before it gets any traction. As we focus on the majesty, power and eternity of our God and Father, even our most extravagant and bold requests are entirely fitting. He is a great God and we acknowledge this by bringing him great requests. The doxology seals the petitions we have just prayed with faith. It secures them in perfect proportion to who God is, leaving us exhilarated with faith and celebrating his great kingdom. We go on our way rejoicing.

THE KINGDOM

The threefold praise of "Yours is the kingdom, the power and the glory", powerfully reminds us that our God is seated in heaven as the Exalted King over a kingdom that is always increasing, never shaken or threatened. His kingdom abounds with all that we need on earth; where he rules there is no shortage or lack of resources. Everything we have asked him for in the petitions of the prayer, he has at his fingertips to grant. We have gone right to the source, to the highest authority in the universe.

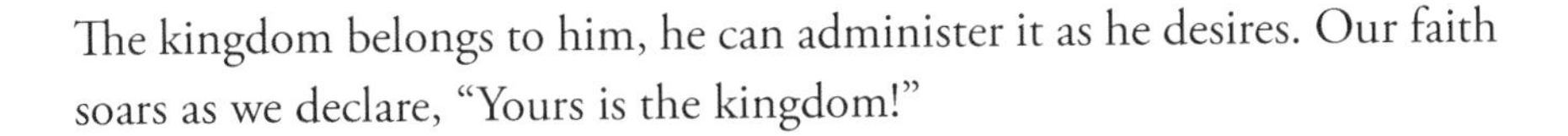

The kingdom belongs to him, he can administer it as he desires. Our faith soars as we declare, "Yours is the kingdom!"

THE POWER

We continue on and now proclaim that in addition to reigning in absolute authority over his kingdom, he has all power. His power is without limits, his ability has no restrictions. He has pledged his power, the mighty arm of God, to the primary task of building his Church. Whatever he chooses to do will be victorious, filled with resurrection power, so as the Church is built, the very gates of hell will not be able to hold back its glorious advance. Jesus will unite her and dwell in her with the fullness of his presence, no matter how fractured she is now. His power will resurrect the dead and Jesus will be revealed in the splendour of his never-fading majesty so that every knee will spontaneously bow in awe. He has the full power to accomplish all that he began, all that he has set in motion. As we align with his will in intercession and lean into his purposes and desires, we are joining in this glorious momentum of advancing the kingdom to its final climax of Christ's return.

What an honour to join the throng that through the ages and across the nations have prayed the Lord's Prayer! Some have prayed it gripped with vision and deep longing, others have prayed the Lord's Prayer from a simple desire to be obedient, unaware of the magnitude of what they were touching. But every prayer, small and struggling or bursting with faith and blazing revelation, adds to this chorus—the Church's Prayer, the Prayer of All Prayers.

THE GLORY

The doxology also proclaims that the glory is God's. This is both a beautiful moment of praise and also a commitment that as our prayers are answered, the Lord will receive the glory, not us.

At times, as we pray for dire situations and needs in our journey through the Lord's Prayer, these burdens remain with us, weighing heavily upon our hearts. We are left troubled and concerned. But the doxology lifts this heaviness. We find ourselves declaring that God's kingdom, power and glory is forever and ever and suddenly the reality of eternity reframes these struggles as "momentary, light, afflictions."[130] Even the most severe persecution or heart-wrenching struggle for a believer can only last a lifetime. A human life in comparison with eternity is a fleeting vapour.

For the early Church, the reality of the resurrection re-defined life and shifted their perspective to one shaped by eternity. They had seen Jesus in his resurrected body, witnessed him ascend to heaven and heard his promise to return to reign as King forever. His resurrection was the guarantee of their resurrection and their confidence in this was the source of their zeal and courage. It was why Paul found himself torn between the option of going to be with the Lord or remaining to serve the Church. Both were highly attractive to him, because his primary focus was on the return of Christ and the great resurrection.

The early Church lost precious friends, brothers and sisters to martyrdom. For them, the concept of the cloud of witnesses was deeply comforting, not in a Hallmark-card kind of way, but in the realization that they couldn't lose even if they were killed. These witnesses who had lost their lives are a part of the "Our" that opened the prayer; they were still very much part of the family, surrounding and cheering those who were still running the race of this life.

Reflecting on the tremendous sacrifice that saints throughout the centuries have made for the kingdom of God encourages us to run well. In a very real sense, we are in the company of those who have done the most glorious exploits for God, who have paid the highest sacrifices. Should they not inspire us, even provoke us, to run in the same way in our generation?

In times of revival, the reality and immediacy of eternity is restored; worldly achievements, acquisitions and pleasures are looked at through the lens of eternity and weighed accordingly. The perspective

130 2 Cor 4:17

of "working while it is day"—doing all that can be done for the glory of God, the advancement of the gospel and the salvation of souls—takes precedence.[131] Sadly, it's when we drift from Jesus and his gospel in times of coldness and lukewarmness, that the things of this world, along with its cares, completely preoccupy our thinking and consume our energy.

The revelation of eternity is often restored in times of revival. It's as if the veil between this life and the eternal realm becomes thin and gauzy. In the same way, as we pray this revival prayer, we can expect eternity to become more pronounced and shape our priorities.

The last word in the prayer is "Amen", which is much more than a religious way to sign off! It is a vigorous declaration of wholehearted agreement. It is a statement that we are fully invested, fully aligned with these prayers, right to the core of our heart. We have not merely mouthed spiritual sounding words, nor have we been double-minded as we prayed. We are earnest and zealous that the Lord would answer these requests that we have lifted to him. This is the final sealing of the prayer, our hearty amen.

APPLYING IT IN PRAYER

As we come to the conclusion of our journey through the Lord's Prayer, we want to consider some ways to expand the doxology and apply it in our prayers.

- Thank you for what you have already done as we have prayed!
- We declare you are the authority over all, the King of all kings forever
- You have all resources at your fingertips, you are our source
- You are able to do, effortlessly, all that we have just asked—help us to stand in faith

131 Jn 9:4

- Your kingdom is always increasing—give us eyes to see this and stand in faith
- The knowledge of your glory will fill the earth, may it come quickly Lord
- May you receive all the glory from the answers to these prayers
- Bring to us the reality of eternity
- Deliver us from putting too much priority on the temporal
- Let us live like those who went before us, those of whom the world was not worthy
- May these ones, the great cloud of witnesses, inspire us to run well and endure to the end
- We seal this prayer in your name—Amen!

SCRIPTURES TO MEDITATE ON

- Yours is the kingdom—1 Chron 29:11
- Yes and amen—2 Cor 1:20
- Dwell in his house forever—Ps 23:6
- Momentary light affliction—2 Cor 4:16-18
- Your throne, O God—Ps 45:6
- Set your minds on things above—Col 3:2
- Alpha and Omega—Rev 1:8, 22:13

GROUP DISCUSSION QUESTIONS:

1. Share how you feel about the idea that as you pray the Lord's Prayer you are joining into the momentum of the prayer and worship of the historical and global Church.
2. What practical things might change in your life if the Father increased your awareness of eternity?
3. Have you ever experienced an attack of unbelief after you have prayed a bold prayer? Can you see how the doxology would help you stand in faith?

Chapter Thirteen

THE PRAYER OF REVIVAL

Ah, revival.

That golden season of supernatural outpouring that brings the Church back to vibrant life and draws thousands, even millions to saving faith. Reaching for this is the groan and yearning of Christians all around the world. "Lord revive us! Holy Spirit come for the sake of Christ!"

Many of us have studied revival, looking for the keys to how it can come again, but this time, where *we* live, touching all the brokenness and dreary mundaneness of *our* lives. We've examined it biblically and historically. We've repented, we've prayed and fasted, we've prophesied and decreed it to be. We've also preached on it, calling the Church to rise up, return to first love, be zealous, prayerful, bold in witness, strong in faith…

We pray. We believe. We wait.

Yet revival, in its simplest form, is God—with all of who He is—drawing near to us. We are not earning an outpouring of his presence and power with a formula. When he draws near there is a palpable, undeniable increase of his manifest presence; the spiritually sensitive know it, and those who have been spiritually dull become equally aware of its reality. His presence, his nearness, comes loaded with the revelation of who he is and his heart for us, which triggers a profound, multifaceted reaction in the community. How could it not? When he comes near, we see him in truth, rather than the distortions we've believed about him. He touches us, speaks to us and everything changes. The very spiritual climate around us is electric with him.

Suddenly, those that have never really even thought about God are aware of an awakened longing. Those that have been walking in coldness and arrogance suddenly have a fresh sense of the fear of the Lord and their hearts are softened in humility and tenderness toward him. Those that have been flirting with the world or have danced into its arms, now wholeheartedly pursue the beauty of holiness and a single-hearted passion for Jesus. What has been dry, fruitless preaching is now flooded with power and the supernatural presence of God, bearing extraordinary fruit as thousands turn to the cross. These, and more, are all the results of God coming near and supernaturally changing the spiritual climate to one powerfully charged with the awareness of him, his goodness and his invitation to respond.

CANADIAN MANTLES OF REVIVAL

In 2012, the Lord led me to begin working on the book, *Canadian Mantles of Revival.*[132] Initially, the goal was to tell Canada's revival stories so that the Canadian Church could be strengthened in faith. However, as I studied it became clear that there were some important lessons to be learned from our history. We could learn from how men and women of God became catalysts that God moved through, catalysts whose surrendered lives opened the doors of revival in their communities.

What also became clear was there were commonalities to the revivals—they shared similar features. Drilling down to see what triggered revival that had changed the past generations, what became apparent was that all true revival has the gospel at its deepest root.

---

132 Sara Maynard, *Canadian Mantles of Revival,* (Vancouver, BC: Redleaf Prayer, 2015) available through: redleafprayer.org.

Let me repeat that, it's vital: all true revival has the gospel at its deepest root.

THE GOSPEL BRINGS REVIVAL

It's the gospel that brings the change, the life, the power. The gospel is more than just a salvation presentation and much bigger than your sins forgiven or heaven in your future. It's bigger than Jesus being a new-found friend who will help you through life or work miracles in your situation. The gospel is all that Jesus taught, all of who he is, what he's done, what he's doing now and all he brings to us. It's an invitation to full, forever union with him, a union which means dying to all the ways we've independently built our lives apart from him, dying to all the things we've put our faith in (including ourselves) and shifting that full weight of our lives to him alone. He alone becomes our Cornerstone and we build on nothing else. We build by fully believing in him, his character, his word and his work. The gospel is exchanging the old self and self-ways for that which is in Christ, an exchange that becomes our new way of walking, an exchange that leads us into knowing him intimately and having our lives become an echo of his.

The Holy Spirit empowers the gospel and its transformational impact on our lives. He is the One who keeps redirecting our eyes towards Jesus when we get distracted, for it is his greatest desire for the Son to receive glory.[133] This is why, in the times when Jesus is most exalted, the manifest presence of the Holy Spirit markedly increases and becomes supernaturally active. These are often the times of revival.

THE GOSPEL IN THE EARLY CHURCH

Have you ever read the book of Acts and marvelled at the unrelenting zeal of the early disciples? Peter and John took their lives in their hands, defying the council of Jewish elders (the same council of leaders that had

---

133 Jn 16:14

just successfully conspired to have Jesus executed) and proclaimed that they "cannot but speak of what they had seen and heard".[134]

"Cannot but speak?" We don't seem to have that problem! Do you wonder about Paul's life as he blazed an apostolic missionary trail through the Gentile world? Beaten, imprisoned, shipwrecked, misunderstood, stoned, running from lynch mobs, beaten again, carrying the burden of young, vulnerable churches, beaten again…

Paul is featured most prominently in the book of Acts, but he wasn't the only one burning with the gospel, unrelenting in his mission to bring the Good News to the nations. It was the culture of the Church. Paul may have been the most obvious example, but he wasn't alone in this. All the Apostles (except John) were martyred and they weren't alone: from young women to old men, our earliest brothers and sisters were torn by animals, stoned, burnt alive and beheaded because they could not deny this glorious gospel. They could not but speak. They could not but believe.

What if our gospel is actually a faint echo of that which was thundering in the breasts of these early believers? What if it's been so watered down and made so comfortable and 'balanced' that we don't offend anyone and we can be tucked tidily into the irrelevant religious box by our man-centred society? If this is the case, the tragic result is a gospel stripped of its glory and power.

Here's where the Lord's Prayer comes in.

The early Church Fathers considered the Lord's Prayer to be the gospel in a condensed form, that the essence of the entire gospel had been packed into this short prayer. Tertullian[135] taught that *"all the writings of the prophets, evangelists, and apostles as well as all of Jesus' sermons, parables, examples and precepts are 'touched on in the brief compass of a few little words', namely the Lord's Prayer.*"[136] One of the ways that the

134 Acts 4:20

135 Tertullian (ca. 150-225) A prolific theologian, recognized as one of the prominent early Church Fathers.

136 Hammerling, *The Lord's Prayer in the Early Church: the Pearl of Great Price*, 6.

gospel stayed fully known and fully embraced was through the daily practice of praying the Lord's Prayer. One of the ways the hearts of the early Church stayed on fire with revival was also through the daily practice of praying the Lord's Prayer.

Praying the Lord's Prayer can have this same effect on us.

This prayer that Jesus instructed us to pray is also what he will use to revive us, drawing us continually deeper into the gospel—that eternally fruitful root of true revival. Praying the Lord's Prayer will have the same impact on us that it did the early Church. The needs of the human heart are universal and how the gospel transforms hearts is also universal—it applies for all times and in all cultures. If we would lean into the gospel and open our hearts to the Holy Spirit, we too would encounter personal revival as we pray this prayer.

REVIVAL-BIRTHING PRAYER

As I and others have studied historical revivals looking for common features, we see the consistency of the of the gospel being rediscovered but also the priority and prominence of prayer. In times of revival, prayer is ubiquitous on every lip and burning in every heart. We see that extraordinary prayer is the precursor to revival and fervent intercession continues throughout the entire move of God. It's when prayer starts to wane and we begin to rely on our own efforts rather than utter dependence on God, that the Holy Spirit begins to lift. With this in mind, intercessory prayer has always been honoured as essential by the revival-hungry Church.

Prayer for revival while always well-intentioned, hasn't always been biblical or effective. The yearning for a widespread outpouring of the Spirit makes us susceptible to the hollow promise of revival that formulas and short-cuts offer us. Jesus was likewise tempted with short-cuts to power but chose obedience to the Father and the work of the cross. Special prayer gatherings, united decrees or praying with new revelations that aren't centred in the gospel won't lead us to revival, no matter how convincingly they are presented.

What if we simply returned with childlike faith to the prayer Jesus called us to pray and through its framework of petitions and points of surrender we prayed earnestly for revival, allowing it to break and humble and transform our hearts in the process?

How could the one prayer Jesus himself gave us to pray *not* be full of the spirit of revival? If we pray it, led by the Spirit, our prayers will be more effective, more joyous and more fruitful than ever before.

SUSTAINING PRAYER FOR REVIVAL

Prayer for revival requires endurance. It is prayer that truly needs to be sustained over an extended period of time, not just rallied for a one-off prayer meeting. Revival prayer is genuine spiritual birthing and staying engaged in that birthing isn't easy. As you pray for nation-shaking revival, even small beginnings of outpouring are partial answers that fuel your endurance. These answers are like the water stations packed with cheering onlookers as you run your marathon. They refresh and invigorate you to keep going. Because the Lord's Prayer is prayer that is well-answered, praying it sustains this flow of encouragement in wonderful ways.

But it's not just the answers. When the presence and affirmation of the Holy Spirit rests upon your intercession, there is a sublime, undeniable partnering that happens. You are with him in his intercession, partnering with him in his works on earth, even if you never personally see the answer with your own eyes. Both the answers and the affirmation of heaven increase as you pray the Lord's Prayer, for it aligns your prayer with his desire and his gospel.

Because the Lord's Prayer is essentially a corporate prayer rather than an individual one, it is the best format that we can use for corporate, united, revival prayer meetings. All that we've experienced personally in our prayer closet can be multiplied through the praying church community. There is no other prayer that can unite us so well or lead us into the same spirit of one accord that the early Church enjoyed, the one accord that the Spirit fell upon with fire.

Returning to the Lord's Prayer as the primary way we pray for revival is a bold statement of our belief in Jesus. It's saying that we believe his character is so good, that his heart is so for us, that he's going to give us the path to pray for revival because he's more intensely invested in revival than any of us could ever be. It's trusting that he desires we be revived and for his power and presence to break into our communities much, much, more than we do.

> *Indeed, he who did not spare his own Son, but gave him up for us all—how will he not also, along with him, freely give us all things?*
> *Rom 8: 32 (NET)*

GROUP DISCUSSION QUESTIONS:

1. Discuss the ways that praying the Lord's Prayer, personally and corporately, leads the Church to revival.
2. Reflect back on the previous chapters and identify which of the petitions or calls to surrender in the Lord's Prayer would most lead to a revived Church.
3. Do you feel your understanding of the gospel is as rich and full as the understanding the early Church had? If not, how could that change?

Appendix i

GETTING STARTED

For those who began this book with a measure of skepticism at my assertion that the Lord's Prayer could be a path to revived communion and life in God, I trust you have been satisfied. I trust that as you have looked more closely at the prayer through the chapters of this book you have become fully convinced that it was indeed designed by Jesus to be the centrepiece of every disciple's prayer life. I trust as well that you have been freshly inspired with the richness and depth of the prayer and are now anticipating it awakening your prayer life with new vibrancy.

Further, I pray that you have caught the vision of the prayer's potential to daily disciple your heart and life in the gospel, a discipling which produces Christlikeness. This means you will become like Jesus in his character, exhibiting the fruit and power of the Spirit that flowed through his life, but also like him in the beauty of his prayer life.

But I would be remiss to leave you at this point without helping transition the concepts of this book into action for those who have not prayed this way before. It's not enough to be convinced or even inspired; we need steps forward—practical, doable steps. We all know that without this, all our good intentions and even a fresh perspective quickly fade as the pressures of life march on. Let's map out some ways this prayer can become part of your daily life.

PRAY IT PERSONALLY

I've said repeatedly through this book that the kingdom of God begins in the heart and when God changes a life, he does so through a person's heart. With this in mind, the beginning place to pray the Lord's Prayer and make it a part of your life is to apply it in prayer to yourself, to your own heart. Think of this like the instructions that the airlines give us for applying our oxygen mask if there is a cabin decompression. We put our mask on first, then help others.

The very first step is to pray the Lord's Prayer, applied to yourself, daily. Below is a simple illustration of how one could pray it through. Here we're imagining a person who is growing spiritually, yet still has some struggles and sins that they are praying about. Your prayer could look something like this.

Our Father who is in heaven

- *Thank you for adopting me and honouring me with being part of such a wonderful family*
- *Help me to trust you in all the areas of anxiety and insecurity that rise up, so I can believe more deeply that you are a good Father*

Hallowed be your name.

- *Father, let your name receive glory in my life and through my life*
- *Help me speak words of life that reflect your nature and love, so that you would gain honour and glory through my words*

Your kingdom come

- *Increase your kingdom activity in my life, let me be a conduit for supernatural blessing to those around me; use me Lord!*

Your will be done on earth as it is in heaven.

- *I yield to you my plans and desires. I surrender to your will for my life and ask for grace in every place where this feels like a wrestle*
- *Today, help me to be yielded and patient where your timing and my timing don't line up*

Give us this day our daily bread.

- *Father, you said you would fill the hungry with good things (Ps 107:9), would you awaken a fresh hunger for Jesus in my heart*
- *Bring me into deeper and greater encounter and intimacy with your Son, the Bread of Heaven*

Forgive us our trespasses

- *Thank you that you've shown me where self-righteousness has risen in my heart. I humbly repent for this. Forgive me Father, and wash me from this sin*

As we forgive those who have trespassed against us.

- *I forgive those who have rejected me and misunderstood me in recent days*
- *Let my heart be free of any flicker of resentment or hesitation to reach out to them again*

Lead us not into temptation

- *Father, you see where I am weak, strengthen me in those places that I'm struggling*
- *May my life become full of overcoming so that you'll be glorified*

But deliver us from the evil one.

- *Protect me from every snare the enemy has set for me*

Yours is the kingdom, the power and the glory, for ever and ever, amen.

Praying the prayer through in this manner would take only a few minutes and would be a great way to start. Once accustomed to the structure, you can naturally expand into much more lengthy times of prayer. You'll find that instead of wondering how to fill your prayer time, you start wondering how to get more time for prayer as it bubbles up and overflows.

The greatest challenge when beginning is remembering to pray it regularly. So here are a few ways to keep up the consistency until praying the Lord's Prayer becomes a habit:

- Use it to close your morning devotions
- Choose a daily prayer time that works for you and set the alarm on your smartphone to remind you
- Pray it while you take the dog for his evening walk
- Leave for work ten minutes early and upon arrival, take time to pray in your car before beginning your day
- Give the Lord the first twenty minutes of your baby's nap time to pray the Lord's Prayer
- Many other ways you might think of!

PRAY IT FOR OTHERS

Once you have built a daily habit of praying the Lord's Prayer, where you apply it to your own life, allow the Lord to draw you into intercession for others. Referring back to our analogy of the oxygen mask—this is where we help someone else get their mask on! The Lord will enlarge your heart with compassion and concern for those around you; your family, your church community, work associates and your neighbourhood. He may bring to mind people that you've not thought of for years and give you an urging to pray for them. At times the whole city or nation could be your burden in prayer. You will find that ten to fifteen minutes (if that's where you began) quickly stretches into forty-five minutes, an hour or even longer. As you intercede for others, be careful not to avoid applying the prayer to your life. It can be tempting to skip over some of the discipling aspects of the Lord's Prayer, setting our focus exclusively on how God can change and help others, while crowding out the space the Lord wants to use to minister to our hearts personally.

To help get you started in a regular discipline of praying the Lord's Prayer, I've added some journal pages at the end of this book, as a place to jot down how you've prayed. Under each phrase from the prayer, make some notes of how the Lord led you to pray. Many people find the activity of journaling while they pray a very helpful way to curb wandering thoughts and maintain focus. Try it out here and if helpful, continue this practice in a full-sized journal. Keeping a brief record of your prayers is also an excellent way to see how faithfully the Father answers.

Another practice that many people find helpful to maintain focus and escape distractions is to pray out loud while going for a walk. Hearing your own voice grabs your attention and the activity of walking energizes your prayer.

PRAYING IT WITH OTHERS

Throughout the book, we've primarily approached the Lord's Prayer as a part of our "closet prayer"—the prayer we do in a private place. But the Lord's Prayer doesn't need to remain there. Remember, it's the prayer that Jesus gave to the whole Church and is a powerful unifier. Praying the Lord's Prayer should not just be the centrepiece of our personal prayer life, but should be utilized in our corporate prayer times. In Redleaf Prayer, the ministry where I serve, we currently host daily intercession times using the format of the Lord's Prayer to intercede for revival in Canada. Each one of these prayer meetings is attended by individuals from a wide variety of different denominations. The centrality of the Lord's Prayer makes it easy for all of us to flow together in prayer. We also use the Lord's Prayer as a structure for larger city-wide interdenominational prayer gatherings.

SOME NUTS AND BOLTS

If you are considering launching a new prayer meeting or reorienting an existing one around the Lord's Prayer, here are a few of the ways we have done it. These approaches can easily be modified to suit your setting.

Leading in a church prayer meeting

Using the Lord's Prayer as a format for church prayer meetings is a wonderful way to unite and engage the whole congregation. It makes participating in prayer accessible for everyone, be they a new Christian or one who is experienced in intercession. Using this format also promotes awareness of the Lord's Prayer, so that the whole congregation may find its petitions naturally arising in their personal prayer times. This in itself can provide a way for the Holy Spirit to stir, awaken and disciple lives.

You will need a leader. While in a small group, leadership can generally be low-key, as it the group grows in size, a stronger presence of leadership is required. The leader's role is to set the pace, to determine when it is appropriate to move to the next petition of the prayer, inviting others to pray their prayers that relate to that phrase. Leaders also shepherd and protect the flow of prayer, so if another agenda arises, the leader graciously redirects.

To lead well, you want to encourage, even activate others to pray. Your meeting should be a united effort where there is a genuine dynamic of team synergy, leaving everyone declaring, "it's better together!" Corporate prayer is also a perfect place to practice leaning into the Holy Spirit, to grow in a united response to him. In Chapter Two we considered some of the prophetic ways the Holy Spirit leads as we pray the Lord's Prayer. When in a group, it's even more important to notice what the Lord is doing, to make room for the prophetic and revelatory gifts and to follow the oil.

In a church setting it's also very appropriate to integrate worship in the flow of prayer and allow the Lord's Prayer to become the foundation for a harp and bowl style of prayer meeting.

When we use the Lord's Prayer in a congregational prayer meeting, we will typically use a mic at the front beside the leader, so the congregation can come and pray as they feel prompted by the Spirit. To add some variety, we might invite a small team of individuals to lead one of the petitions on behalf of the congregation. While spontaneous, congregational prayer gives everyone the freedom to participate, assigning a few mature individuals one of the petitions brings greater depth to the prayer meeting. Both are important. When we lead in these settings, we try to steward the prayer time, protecting it from everyone's natural tendency towards sharing or even preaching mini-sermons! This is a universal problem, as it's easier to talk to each other than to talk to God.

We also break into small groups of five or six to pray one of the petitions, so everyone has a chance to participate, before regathering for the next part of the prayer. A combination of these different approaches and others you will think of gives everyone a way to participate, allows freedom for the Holy Spirit and keeps the meeting energized.

Another role for the leader is to move the prayer deeper if it seems stuck at a shallow, surface level. At Redleaf, we ask those who are involved in our weekly Lord's Prayer meetings to personally pray the Lord's Prayer daily. This opens for them a rich well, full of revelation and related scriptures that is alive in their hearts. This is a well they can easily draw from as they join into corporate prayer.

If you use the Lord's Prayer as the format for your church prayer meeting, don't be afraid of it getting stale; there will always be new ways to apply it. The Lord's Prayer is a prayer that is expansive enough to carry your corporate prayer life! While using it as a format will require an investment of preparation (as any corporate prayer meeting does) and at times may require digging a bit deeper to find the flow of the Spirit, as you persist, the tremendous fruit makes it worth it all.

Leading city-wide prayer

The larger the gathering of people you are leading in prayer, the greater the need for structure, simplicity and clarity. Investing in careful preparation will enable you to keep even a diverse group united, engaged and understanding where you are going.

For a city-wide or interdenominational prayer meeting, you could use a similar structure as we are suggesting for a congregational prayer meeting, except have a team of leaders who take turns introducing a petition of the prayer, rather than just one prayer leader. Slides, handouts and other tools all contribute to keeping the gathering connected and united. Pastors give confident leadership and it's beautiful to see a group standing together in prayer.

There are a wide variety of effective approaches for city-wide prayer gatherings using the Lord's Prayer. Allow the Lord to inspire you with new ideas that will be just right for your setting. Remember, however, that the goal is not well-structured or perfectly led meetings—it's always faith-filled, Spirit-led, united and biblical prayer!

Finally, pray this prayer! Pray it daily with your whole heart, with all of your faith and passion!

Encourage others to pray it and pray it with them! Keep praying it, don't let it be a passing fad but let it take its rightful place as the Prayer of All Prayers, centring and expanding prayer into the rest of your life.

Appendix ii

JOURNAL YOUR PRAYER

Our Father in Heaven

____

____

____

____

____

Hallowed be Your Name

____

____

____

____

____

Your kingdom come

Your will be done on earth as it is in heaven.

Give us this day our daily bread

Forgive us our trespasses

As we forgive those who trespass against us

Lead us not into temptation,

But deliver us from the evil one.

For Yours is the kingdom, and the power and the glory, for ever and ever, amen.

JOURNAL YOUR PRAYER

Our Father in Heaven

Hallowed be Your Name

Your kingdom come

Your will be done on earth as it is in heaven.

Give us this day our daily bread

Forgive us our trespasses

As we forgive those who trespass against us

Lead us not into temptation,

But deliver us from the evil one.

For Yours is the kingdom, and the power and the glory, for ever and ever, amen.

JOURNAL YOUR PRAYER

Our Father in Heaven

Hallowed be Your Name

Your kingdom come

Your will be done on earth as it is in heaven.

Give us this day our daily bread

Forgive us our trespasses

As we forgive those who trespass against us

Lead us not into temptation,

But deliver us from the evil one.

For Yours is the kingdom, and the power and the glory, for ever and ever, amen.

BIBLIOGRAPHY

Apostolic Fathers *The Didache*, rediscovered in 1873.

Crossan, John Dominic *The Greatest Prayer: Rediscovering the Revolutionary Message of the Lord's Prayer.* New York, New York: Harper Collins Publishers, 2010.

Finney, Charles G. *Revival Lectures.* Old Tappan, New Jersey: Fleming H. Revell Co. Publishers

Hammerling, Roy *The Lord's Prayer in the Early Church.* New York, New York: Palgrave Macmillan, 2010.

Johnson, Darrell W. *Fifty-Seven Words that Change the World: A Journey Through the Lord's Prayer.* Vancouver, British Columbia, Canada: Regent College Publishing, 2005.

Kendall, R. T. *The Lord's Prayer: Insight and Inspiration to Draw You Closer to Him.* Grand Rapids, Michigan: Chosen Books, 2010.

Lea, Larry *Could You Not Tarry One Hour? Learning the Joy of Prayer.* Altamonte Springs, Florida: Creation House, 1987.

Litfin, Bryan *Getting to Know the Church Fathers: an Evangelical Introduction.* Grand Rapids, Michigan: Baker Academic Publishing, 2007.

Luther, Martin *Lord, Teach Us to Pray: Martin Luther's Exposition of the Lord's Prayer.* Public Domain from Martin Luther's Large Catechism.

Ortberg, John *The Lord's Prayer: Praying with Power.* Grand Rapids, Michigan: Zondervan, 2008.

Packer, J.I. *Praying the Lord's Prayer* (Wheaton, Illinois: Crossway Books, 2007).

Ryken, Philip Graham *When You Pray—Making the Lord's Prayer Your Own.* Wheaton, Illinois: Crossway Books, 2000.

Stewart-Sykes, Alistair *Tertullian, Cyprian, Origen, On the Lord's Prayer.* Crestwood, New York: St Vladimir's Seminary Press, 2004.

Stott, John *The Message of the Sermon on the Mount.* Downers Grove, Illinois: Inter-Varsity Press, 1978.

Sproul, R. C. *The Prayer of the Lord.* Lake Mary, Florida: Reformation Trust, 2009.

Wright, N. T. *The Lord and His Prayer.* Grand Rapids, Michigan: William B Eerdmans Publishing Co., 1996.

Acknowledgments

As the vision for this book grew, so did the enthusiastic cadre of friends who God sent to carry it with me. Their help, coming in many different forms, was invaluable. Some faithfully prayed while others helped underwrite the cost of getting the book to press and still others kept a steady stream of prophetic encouragement coming my way. I am deeply thankful for this support. So: Teena Ferrara, Redleaf Prayer, Wanda and Lawrence Kopp, Via Apostolica, Bryan Elliot, and of course, Mike, my steadfast husband, thank you!

In addition, specific thanks goes to those who edited or who worked through the book's theology with me. These ones have put some real skin in the game. Chad Block, Brant Levert, Richard Long, Chris Wright and Melinda Appenheimer—you have each invested long hours at high personal cost. Thank you for your friendship and for thoroughly believing in this project.

Thanks are also due to Bishop Todd Atkinson and the Via clergy who spent years wrestling out the robust, good gospel that runs through Corpus Christi, Via Apostolica's flagship discipleship course. I hope you can hear the echoes of what you have taught resonate through these pages.

Finally, thanks go to Jesus who has enabled the writing and the praying and who crafted this Prayer of All Prayers as a glorious and generous gift to his people.

Soli Deo Gloria

About the Author

Sara Maynard is a Canadian prayer leader who has served in the leadership of regional and national prayer ministries since 2000. After her years as the Director of the Vancouver House of Prayer, she established Redleaf Prayer, a national ministry that God has used to mobilize, unite and strengthen prayer in Canada, particularly with a focus of revival and harvest. She continues to serve as Redleaf's Executive Director.

Sara is also the founder and Chair of the Ears to Hear Network of Canadian Prayer Ministries, a group that builds relationship between established prayer ministries for the purpose of support, encouragement and regularly discerning what God is saying to the nation. This value of discerning what God is saying is vital for Spirit-led prayer. A nation the size of Canada has great potential for isolation and regionalism. Ears to Hear seeks to overcome these trends and build national unity.

Although Sara serves in para-church leadership, she has a deep conviction that the local church is God's primary building block for kingdom activity. All her teaching reflects this value.

Sara is the author of *Canadian Mantles of Revival*, nine stories of Canada's greatest revivals, and what we can learn from them, published in 2015. She is also a wife, mother and a grandmother. Sara and her husband Mike attend Via Apostolica (Vancouver), where she serves in intercessory leadership.

To inquire about Sara speaking at your event
please email: info@redleafprayer.org

For additional information: redleafprayer.org

For information about Ears to Hear: ears2hear.ca

THE CATHEDRAL LIBRARY

From the earliest days, a cathedral was to be a light to a city, a region and potentially even a nation. It existed to give support to local parishes wherever possible and the individuals who are a part of them.

The Cathedral Library is seeking to carry on this tradition in the digital age. Content is developed within a local church context for the sake of all local churches and the people who worship there.

Our dream is that The Cathedral Library would bless everyone that accesses our content, in whatever way they choose to employ it. Whether that be for yourself, your family and friends, your community, your ministry, or your local church - we welcome you to do so! Everything we can give away for free, we do. The Cathedral Library aims to be a blessing to everyone; we hope that includes you!

A part of Via Apostolica Church Canada.

www.cathedrallibrary.com

Made in the USA
Columbia, SC
12 January 2019